Personal Historian 2

The Companion Guide

or

How to Write Your Personal History and Live to Tell About It

by

Michael T. Booth

RootsMagic, Inc.
PO Box 495
Springville, Utah 84663
USA

International Standard Book Number: 978-1-932932-16-4

Printed in the United States of America

Trademarks

About the Author

Michael T. Booth is vice-president of RootsMagic, Inc., and the author of the *Personal Historian* software. He is an accomplished trainer, having given hands-on entertaining presentations to thousands of individuals. With over 35 years of computer programming experience, he is also a developer of the popular *RootsMagic* genealogy software. Michael lives in South Ogden, Utah with his wife, Sandy and their six children.

Dedication

I dedicate this book to my dad, Gordon- whose words and ideas are woven throughout every page; to my mom, June- who still teaches me the importance of both family and history; and to my wife, Sandy- who is my co-author and cohort in our own stories and adventures.

Table of Contents

Introduction

Why you need *Personal Historian*

You sit down at your computer and open your word processor. A large, blank page glares at you- daring you to blacken it with your keystrokes. Assessing the challenge, you enthusiastically begin typing. A single word, "Birth", appears on the screen. "So far, so good," you think to yourself. With a little less certainty, your fingers manage to type in a date, a place, and a few names. "Now what?" you ask yourself.

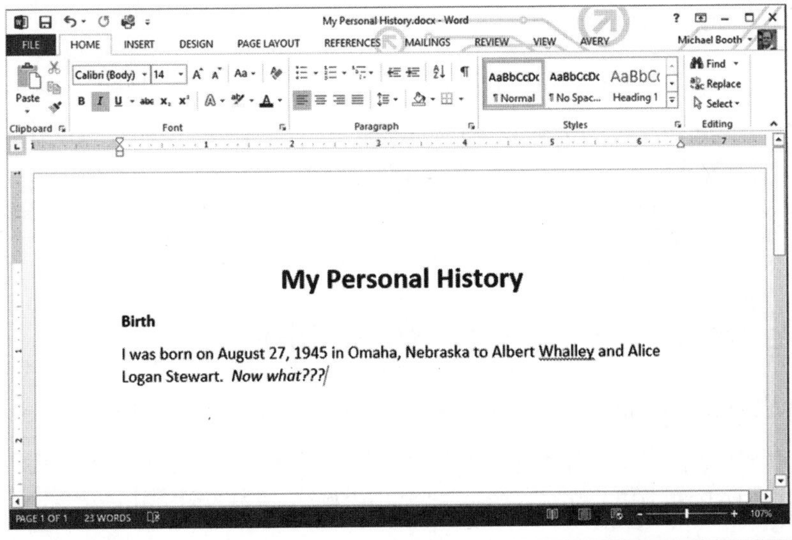

Suddenly the enormity of the task hits you like that foul ball in the 3rd grade. You fumble through a few more paragraphs before deciding that you would do better retreating, regrouping, and charging the enemy at a later time.

Promising yourself that you will return someday, your hand defeatedly clicks on the "Save" button and the once-blank page, although scarred with a few sentences, triumphantly disappears.

Sound familiar? If so, you're not alone. Many people want to write a personal history about themselves or a family member, but they just become lost or overwhelmed by the size and complexity of the project. That's where *Personal Historian* comes in.

What is *Personal Historian*?

Personal Historian is unique computer software that helps you write the story of your life and that of other individuals. It takes this seemingly monumental task and breaks it into small, manageable pieces and then reconstructs it into a complete, publishable document.

From start to finish, *Personal Historian* is the quickest, easiest, and most enjoyable way to write your personal history or that of someone else. You'll be amazed at how easy and entertaining it can be.

Personal Historian's History

In 2003, my parents and I were discussing personal histories. This wasn't a completely new topic for us. Gordon and June had both spent many years researching their genealogies and had instilled in me a love for family history from an early age. We had attended several classes and even had some books on the subject of writing your life stories.

My parents both wanted to write not only their personal histories but the histories of my grandparents, all of whom had already passed away.

We were all quite familiar with how computers had made recording genealogy so much easier than the old days of pen and paper. We assumed that somebody must have already tackled the "personal history problem" with technology, and I set out to find the solution.

In my quest, I found plenty of software which helped you write a journal, write a novel, make a scrapbook, or answer interview questions. But I couldn't find anything specifically designed to address the unique challenges of writing a life narrative.

So I decided to make my own.

Easier said than done. It took many months and long days of designing, programming, testing, and doing it all over again. More than once I had to scrap an idea and go back to the drawing board. But we knew we were on to something.

Finally, in the spring of 2004, *Personal Historian* was born, and the public first started using it. It's been very gratifying to watch it grow and evolve thanks to the support and feedback of thousands of users. I love hearing stories about how the software has helped people finally make progress on their histories and to see the amazing stories they have been able to capture with it.

The truth is, despite the benefit that it has been to others, I made *Personal Historian* for purely personal, selfish reasons.

And one of those reasons became a reality on January 13, 2015. That's the day that my dad passed away.

As we were grieving and making preparations for his funeral, I was asked to put together a life sketch that would be read by one of his grandchildren. So I booted up his laptop and opened up *Personal Historian*.

There they were. Stories of his life- in his words and with his voice. Funny anecdotes, sensitive feelings, and a lifetime of lessons learned. Priceless treasures left for us and generations to come.

Whatever benefit it is to others, this software has already given my family and me an invaluable gift. My hope is that *Personal Historian* will help you make your own priceless treasures.

About this Book

"User Manual" is such an unfriendly word. I've tried to make this book much more than a cold, technical description of just another computer application. Because a personal history should be much more than a lifeless description of events, I wanted this book to be a little more colorful and have a little more personality.

Yes, you will find the expected technical descriptions and walk-throughs. But, hopefully, you'll also find practical tips, new ideas, and needed inspiration to finally bring life to your life stories.

Why you can't write your personal history

Why are you doing this?

You've bought this book, which tells me that you are at least *interested* in writing a personal history. But have you really asked yourself, *why* you're writing a personal history? It reminds me of Alice's exchange with the Cheshire Cat in Lewis Carroll's, *Alice in Wonderland*:

> *"Would you tell me, please, which way I ought to go from here?"*
>
> *"That depends a good deal on where you want to get to," said the Cat.*
>
> *"I don't much care where–" said Alice.*
>
> *"Then it doesn't matter which way you go," said the Cat.*

If you don't know "where" you want to go with a personal history, then the other details such as "how," "when", or even "if" don't matter.

Ask yourself, "What purpose will this personal history serve?"

Some people may wish to write only as a creative exercise. Others may write as a therapeutic way to work through past experiences. Many write as a way to leave a connection with future generations.

I once met a gentleman who volunteered at a prison, helping inmates research their own family histories. He told me that the rehabilitation rate for those in his program was among the highest in the system.

The reason? Many of those incarcerated said that they had previously felt alone and adrift. After researching their family histories, they realized that they were actually the culmination of generations of men and women, just like them. Men and women who had also struggled, sacrificed, and overcome.

The connection to their past had changed their present lives and would forever influence their futures.

For me, I record my life stories not out of a sense of vanity, self-importance, or ego. I write because I want my children and grandchildren to know who I was. Maybe they'll see that we share some interests or personality traits. Maybe they'll learn from my experiences and avoid mistakes that I made. Maybe the connection that I leave for them will give them strength to overcome their own challenges in life.

> Whatever your reason for writing a personal history, make sure that you define it clearly in your mind before you start writing.

After all, knowing where you want to go will tell you how to get there.

The obstacles

I've worked with many people trying to write personal histories and have taught many classes on the subject. In my classes, I often ask, "How many of you have started writing a personal history?"

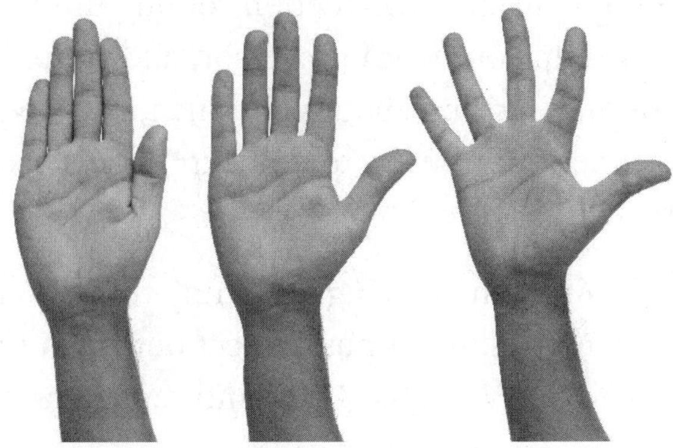

Most of the hands go up.

Next I ask, "How many of you have finished or caught up writing the history?"

Most of the hands go down.

In my experience, most people **want** to write a personal history. If not their own, one for somebody important to them as a way of preserving their memory. But for all those who want to write a life story, very few are successful.

As I've discussed it with them, I've found some common obstacles that prevent one from successfully completing a personal history:

1. I don't know where to start
2. I don't have the time
3. I can't remember enough details
4. I'm not a good writer

Throughout this book, I'm going to show you how *Personal Historian* is specially designed to help you overcome each of these obstacles.

"I don't know where to start"

Did that example in the introduction sound familiar? Have you just opened up your word processor, and started at the (literal) beginning writing about your birth, only to get lost and overwhelmed about what to do next? That's because you started at the wrong place.

The human brain is an amazing yet funny thing. When we're writing our memories, we almost expect our brain to work like a DVD player. We press "Play" and re-watch the movie of our life from beginning to end.

While stories and movies are organized chronologically, our memories aren't. We recall memories in an almost random order, triggered by the smallest of things- a song on the radio, an old friend we bump into, or a familiar smell as we enter a kitchen.

And yet we often try to record these memories chronologically and wonder why they don't come rushing back to us.

Personal Historian solves this problem for you. It creates a timeline of your life, allowing you to see all the important events in your life. Then you simply add stories to this timeline, writing the stories in whatever order you want. It takes care of the organization for you.

For more help getting started, look at these sections:

- "Getting started" on page 13

- "The Main Screen" on page 37

"I don't have the time"

Many people think that to write a personal history, they'll have to spend a month in a hotel room, isolated from the world and free of all distractions.

Life is busy. After taking care of all of the things that we must do, there are still so many worthwhile things that we want to do. So finding that month of isolation seems downright impossible. If this sounds familiar, then you need to rethink your approach.

It's like the old saying: "How do you eat an elephant?" The answer, "One bite at a time."

Focusing on a giant, comprehensive story of your life is like trying to eat the elephant all at once. Instead, break it down into something more bite-sized.

> Focus on writing small, manageable **stories**. Individual stories are much less intimidating, and you can write them in just a few minutes carved out of each day.

Best of all, you don't have to wait until you've written a 400-page tome to feel like you've accomplished something. Every time you finish writing a simple story you'll get a nice sense of accomplishment. That, in turn, motivates you to do it again. And again. And again.

Personal Historian makes it easy to quickly write these individual stories, no matter how much time you have. Before you know it, these little bites add up. *Personal Historian* will then pull the stories together into a single book for you.

Voila! The elephant is eaten.

For more help working with stories, look at these sections:

- "Managing Your Stories" on page 63
- "The Editor Screen" on page 87
- "Putting It All Together" on page 141

"I can't remember enough details"

This one can be harder to admit than we'd like. Sometimes we put off writing our stories because our memory isn't as sharp or as reliable as it used to be.

The good news is that hope is not lost. *Personal Historian* has many tools to help you dig into the past and recover those lost memories and details. From timelines and LifeCapsules to the Organizer and brainstorming, you'll be amazed and excited as your once-fractured memory starts coming together again.

For help getting started, look at these sections:

- "Importing LifeCapsules & Timelines" on page 27
- "The Memory Solution" on page 99

"I'm not a good writer"

OK, so not everybody is an Ernest Hemingway or J.K. Rowling. That's not a problem unless you're planning to write an award-winning novel.

The great thing about personal histories is that the audience is very forgiving. If you've had the blessing of reading a history, journal, or even a letter left by a loved one or ancestor, you understand that grammar or writing ability do not diminish their value.

For help with your writing, look at these sections:

- "How to Write Good" on page 125
- "Do I Have Your Attention?" on page 135

Getting started

Let's walk through setting up a new *Personal Historian* file. The software uses a very easy step-by-step wizard to guide you through this process.

> You must create a new file for each history that you're writing. However, you can create as many files as you want.

For example, I have a file for myself and my wife has her own file. I have a file for each of my kids that I use to record stories on their behalf. I have several other files for ancestors that I'm writing about. I even have a file for an organization that I belong to for which I maintain a history.

In this example, we'll just pretend we're setting up a file for our own history.

The Welcome Screen

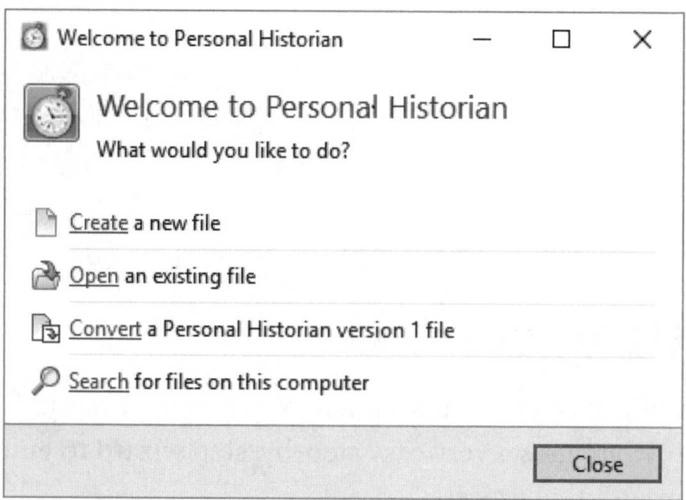

When you open *Personal Historian*, you'll be greeted with the "Welcome Screen". This screen gives you several options to get started.

> **Create a new file** – This makes a new *Personal Historian* file.
>
> **Open an existing file** – Open a previously-created *Personal Historian* file to work on an existing history.
>
> **Convert a *Personal Historian* version 1 file** – If you're one of the lucky users who has been using *Personal Historian* since version 1, use this option to open and convert it into a *Personal Historian* 2 file.
>
> **Search for files on this computer** – If you're like most people and can't keep track of every file on your computer, use this option to display a list of all *Personal Historian* files on your system.

Let's click on **Create a new file**. The "Create a New File" wizard will appear.

Creating a new file

You can create a new *Personal Historian* file by clicking **Create a new file** from the Welcome Screen, clicking the New File icon on the Toolbar, or selecting **File** > **New** from the Main Menu.

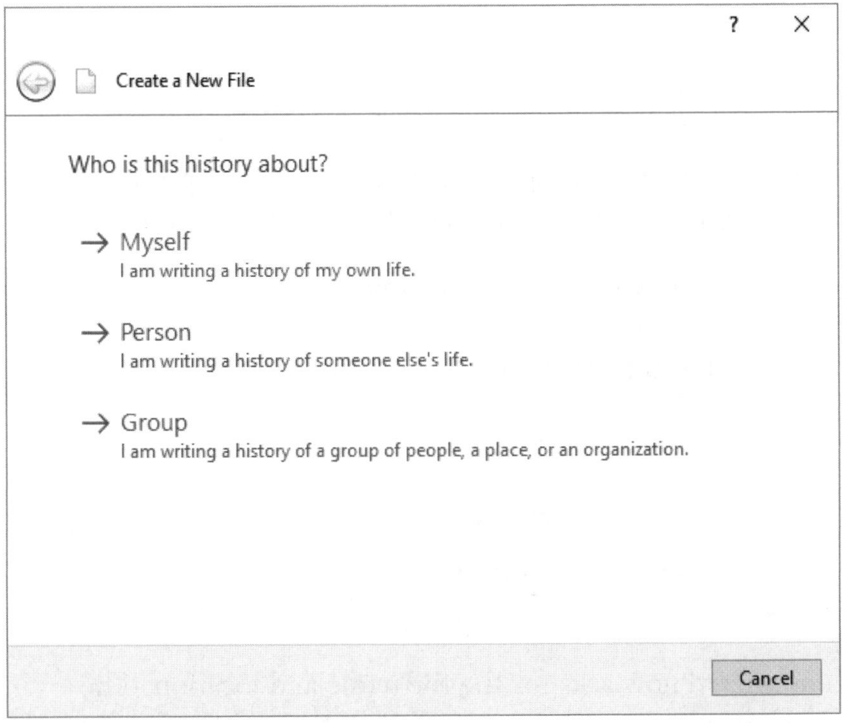
?
Create a New File
Who is this history about?
Myself
I am writing a history of my own life.
Person
I am writing a history of someone else's life.
Group
I am writing a history of a group of people, a place, or an organization.
Cancel

The step-by-step wizard will appear and walk you through the creation of your new file.

▶ Who is this history about?

The first step is to tell *Personal Historian* about your subject. Your choices are:

Myself – I am writing a history of my own life.

Person – I am writing a history of someone else's life.

Group – I am writing a history of a group of people, a place, or an organization.

For this example, click **Myself**.

▶ What is your name?

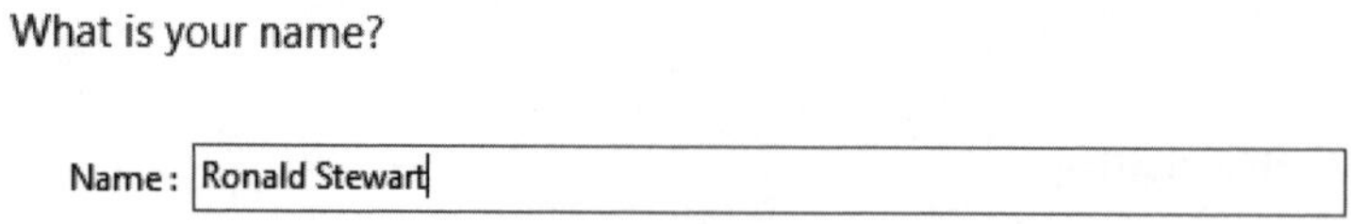

What is your name?

Name : Ronald Stewart

You will then be prompted to enter your name or the name of the person or group that is the subject of the history.

Enter the name and then click **Next**.

▶ Choose a filename for the new file

Choose a filename for the new file

New Filename : Ronald Stewart.phist

Location : C:\Users\Mike\Documents

Change Location

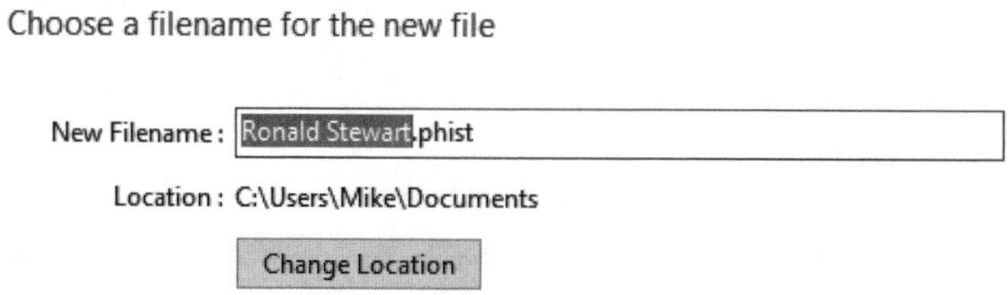

The wizard now asks for the file name and location. The default location will be your computer's "Documents" folder. You may change this by clicking **Change Location**.

Change the default filename and location if desired. Click **Create File** when ready.

▶ Import Genealogy

The next step in setting up your new file is to import genealogy data.

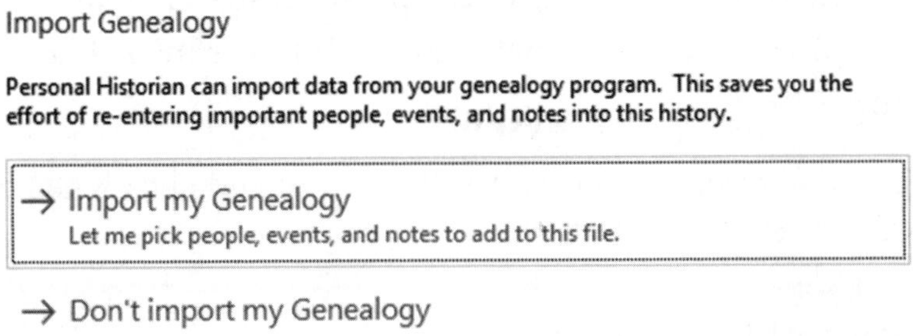

Import Genealogy

Personal Historian can import data from your genealogy program. This saves you the effort of re-entering important people, events, and notes into this history.

→ Import my Genealogy
Let me pick people, events, and notes to add to this file.

→ Don't import my Genealogy

If you use genealogy software such as *RootsMagic*, you've already spent some time entering names, relationships, dates, places, and possibly even stories, notes, and pictures into it. Much of this information may be useful for your writing. Importing this data saves you the effort of re-entering important people, events, and notes into the history.

This step is optional. To skip this step, click **Don't import my Genealogy**. You can always import it later by selecting **File** > **Import** > **Import Genealogy** from the Main Menu.

If you have data that you'd like to import, click **Import my Genealogy**. See the section "Importing Genealogy" on page 21 for a detailed look at this step.

▶ More About You

The next step is to add more information about the history's subject. The information varies depending on whether you are writing about yourself, another person, or a group.

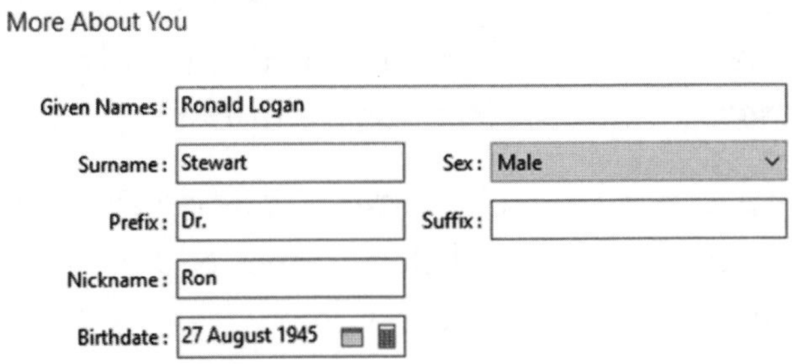

More About You

Given Names: Ronald Logan
Surname: Stewart Sex: Male
Prefix: Dr. Suffix:
Nickname: Ron
Birthdate: 27 August 1945

If you imported genealogy in the previous step, *Personal Historian* will use that information to fill in as many blanks as it can.

Add and correct any relevant information and click **Next** to proceed.

▶ Import LifeCapsules

The next step in setting up your new file is to import LifeCapsules.

Import LifeCapsules

Personal Historian comes with a wide variety of "LifeCapsules"- packaged sets of timelines, events, prompts, and memory triggers that assist you in writing a personal history.

→ Import some LifeCapsules
Let me pick timelines and memory triggers to add to this file.

→ Don't import any LifeCapsules

LifeCapsules are packaged sets of timelines, events, prompts, and memory triggers that assist you in writing a personal history. *Personal Historian* comes with a large library of LifeCapsules covering timelines like "U.S. History", "Inventions", "Epidemics", "Movies", and much more. They are incorporated into your Story List (timeline) giving you valuable context and reminding you of important dates and events.

This step is optional. To skip it, click **Don't import any LifeCapsules**. You can always import one later by selecting **File** > **Import** > **Import LifeCapsule** from the Main Menu.

If you'd like import one, click **Import some LifeCapsules**. See the section "Importing LifeCapsules & Timelines" on page 27 for a detailed look at this step.

▶ Your new file is ready!

Congratulations! You should now see a message that your new *Personal Historian* file is ready for you to begin writing stories.

Your new file is ready!

Your new file is ready for you to begin writing stories! To write about any story in your list, double-click on it.

To add a new event or story, click "Add Story" on the main toolbar.

Remember, you can import additional information by selecting File > Import from the main menu.

Click **Done** to close the wizard and return to the Main Screen (see page 37). Now the *real* magic begins!

Importing Data

Importing Genealogy

Importing your genealogy into *Personal Historian* can be a tremendous time-saver.

If you use genealogy software such as *RootsMagic*, you've already spent some time entering names, relationships, dates, places, and possibly even stories, notes, and pictures into it. Much of this information may be useful for the history that you are writing. Importing this data saves you the effort of re-entering important people, events, and notes into the history.

> If you've already imported your genealogy file into the *Personal Historian* file, it will check for duplicate people and events.
>
> This means that if you've made any changes or additions to your genealogy data, you may re-import it into your *Personal Historian* file to keep it up-to-date.

You can import your genealogy when you create a new file (see page 15) or by selecting **File** > **Import** > **Import Genealogy** from the Main Menu.

The "Import Genealogy" wizard will appear.

▶ Which genealogy software do you use?

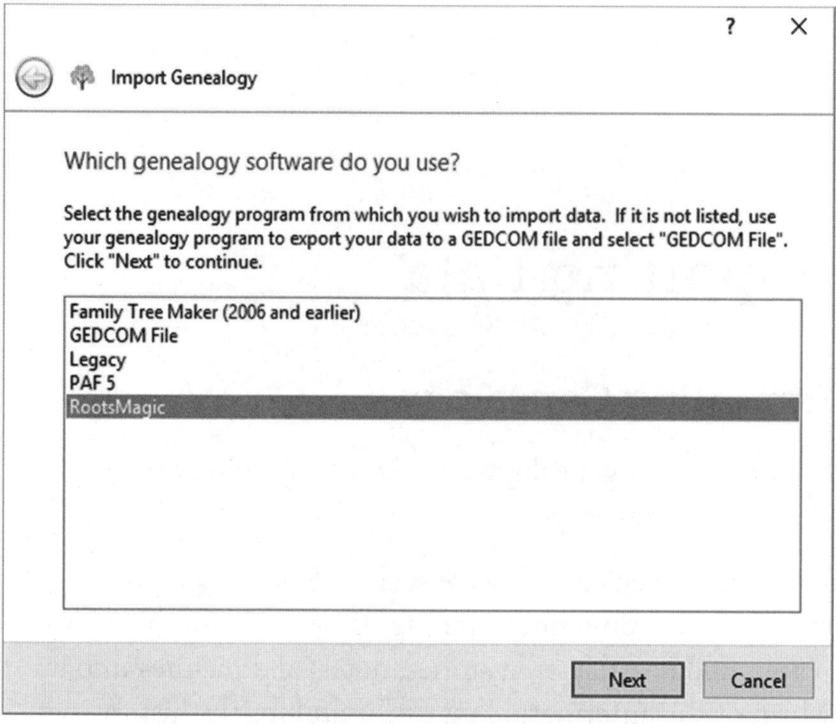

? X
Import Genealogy
Which genealogy software do you use?
Select the genealogy program from which you wish to import data. If it is not listed, use your genealogy program to export your data to a GEDCOM file and select "GEDCOM File". Click "Next" to continue.
Family Tree Maker (2006 and earlier)
GEDCOM File
Legacy
PAF 5
RootsMagic
Next
Cancel

You must first select the genealogy program from which you wish to import data. Your choices include:

- RootsMagic
- Family Tree Maker (2006 and earlier)
- Legacy
- PAF 5

If you don't see your genealogy software listed there, choose "GEDCOM." GEDCOM stands for GEnealogical Data COMmunications, which is a universal format for sharing and transferring genealogical data. Please see your genealogy software's help for instructions on creating a GEDCOM file of your data.

Select your genealogy program and click **Next**.

▶ Where is the file you wish to import?

The wizard now asks if you know where your genealogy file is. Click **I know where the file is** if you do. Click **I'm not sure where the file is** if you're only human and need the software to search your computer for your file.

Where is the file you wish to import?

→ I know where the file is
Let me browse my computer for the file.

→ I'm not sure where the file is
Search my computer for the file.

Select the file you want and then click **Open**.

▶ Who is this history about?

Personal Historian will read the genealogy file and display a list of all the people in it.

Who is this history about?

Select from the list the individual about which you are writing.

Name	Born	Died
Stewart, Matthew Ronald	1983	
Stewart, Melissa	1997	
Stewart, Olivia	2015	
Stewart, Penelope	2013	
Stewart, Ronald Logan	1945	2011
Stewart, Suzanne Lynn	1980	
Stewart, Tyler Kirk	2002	
Stewart, Willard John	1973	
Thomas, Linda	1973	

> You can easily search for a specific person by just typing the name (*Last Name, First Name*).

Select the person that you are writing about from the list and click **Next**.

▶ Which relatives do you wish to import?

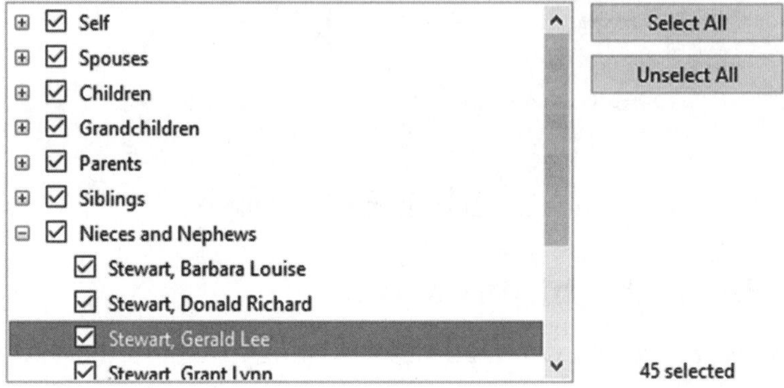

You may now select additional people in the genealogy file to import. This makes sense because events in your relatives' lives likely are an important part of your personal history. For example, when your younger brother was born, when your grandmother died, when your sister was married, etc.

Personal Historian presents a list of relationships, each with a checkbox. Simply check the relationships that you wish to import and uncheck the relationships you want to ignore.

If you want to be more specific, there is a little plus sign next to each relationship. Click on it and it will expand, showing you the names of the relatives, each with a checkbox.

A common mistake is to select all or too many relatives. Doing so will fill the timeline with names and events of distant relatives that aren't important to the personal history.

Don't be afraid to be picky about who you include. Make sure that everyone that you add plays a direct role in the history.

Once you've selected the relatives to import, click **Next**.

▶ Which events do you wish to import?

Now it is time to select which events to import into the Story List.

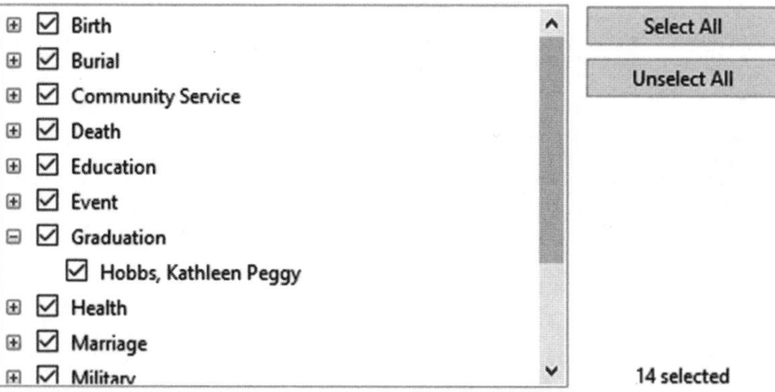

You'll see the list of all event and fact types in your file, each with a checkbox. Simply check the events that you wish to import and uncheck the events you want to ignore.

If you want to be more specific, there is a little plus sign next to each event type. Click on it and it will expand, showing you the names of the people with that event or fact type, each with a checkbox.

> Everyone keeps track of the "classic" vital statistics- birth, death, burial, etc. But don't neglect to record other types of information in your genealogy software. Facts such as "Occupation", "Graduation", and "Physical Description" are incredibly useful in writing personal histories.
>
> Most genealogy software will also allow you to create your own facts and events. (As a southpaw, I like to keep track of "left-handedness".) These are the tidbits that really put the "flesh on the bones", as they say.

Once you've selected the events to import, click **Next**.

▶ Choose Your Options

The last step is to adjust any options before importing the genealogy data.

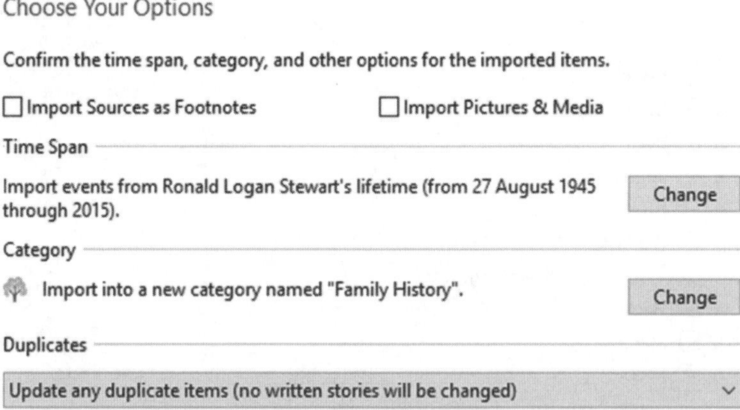
Choose Your Options
Confirm the time span, category, and other options for the imported items.
Import Sources as Footnotes
Import Pictures & Media
Time Span
Import events from Ronald Logan Stewart's lifetime (from 27 August 1945 through 2015).
Change
Category
Import into a new category named "Family History".
Change
Duplicates
Update any duplicate items (no written stories will be changed)

Import Sources as Footnotes – check this to import event sources from the genealogy file. It will add each source as a footnote in the event's story.

Import Pictures & Media – check this to import event pictures and media from the genealogy file. It will add each picture to its story.

Time Span – click **Change** to change the time span of events imported. The default is only to include events from the subject's lifetime.

Category – click **Change** to change the category of the imported stories. The default will be a category named, "Family History".

Duplicates – select what you want to do with any duplicate stories: "Don't import any duplicate items", "Update any duplicate items (no written stories will be changed)", or "Import all duplicate items".

Click **Import** to begin the import and to close the wizard.

Importing LifeCapsules & Timelines

One of the best-loved features of *Personal Historian* is the included library of "LifeCapsules". LifeCapsules are packaged sets of timelines, events, prompts, and memory triggers that assist you in writing a personal history.

They cover a wide variety of topics and timelines such as "U.S. History", "Inventions", "Epidemics", "Movies", and much more. Users can even make their own LifeCapsules to share with others.

> Many LifeCapsules cover many centuries of history, making *Personal Historian* well-suited to writing histories for people who lived in the distant past.

LifeCapsules serve several functions:

1. **Context** – an understanding of world events and culture will help the reader understand an individual's

personal stories and choices.

For example, after incorporating the "Inventions" LifeCapsule into my great-grandfather's history, I could see that he worked as a lineman stringing power lines just a few years after Edison invented the light bulb. What I had previously seen as an ordinary job I could now imagine was an exciting and high-tech job.

2. **Color** – including tidbits of information of what the world was like- including movies, music, and toys- brings the stories to life and makes them more interesting to the reader.

3. **Reminders** – just looking at a timeline of events from your life will immediately spark memories and give you ideas for stories to write; even providing dates and a timeframe for when the story took place.

4. **Prompts and Questions** – some LifeCapsules (especially the "Memory Triggers" LifeCapsule) include prompts and questions that help you write your own history or give you interview questions to ask someone else.

You can import LifeCapsules when you create a new file (see page 27) or by selecting **File** > **Import** > **Import LifeCapsule** from the Main Menu.

The "Import LifeCapsules" wizard will appear.

▶ Which LifeCapsule do you wish to import?

You'll first see a list of available LifeCapsules.

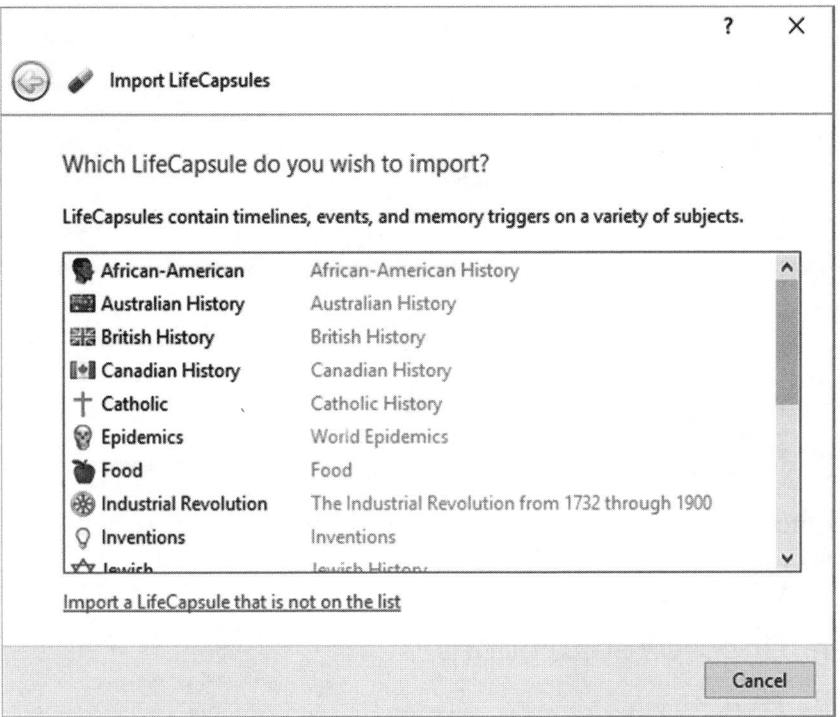

You may choose one from the list or **click Import a LifeCapsule that is not on the list** to choose another one from your computer.

Click **Next** to continue.

▶ What types of items would you like to import?

Some LifeCapsules are sub-divided into smaller groups, allowing you to specify which types of items to import.

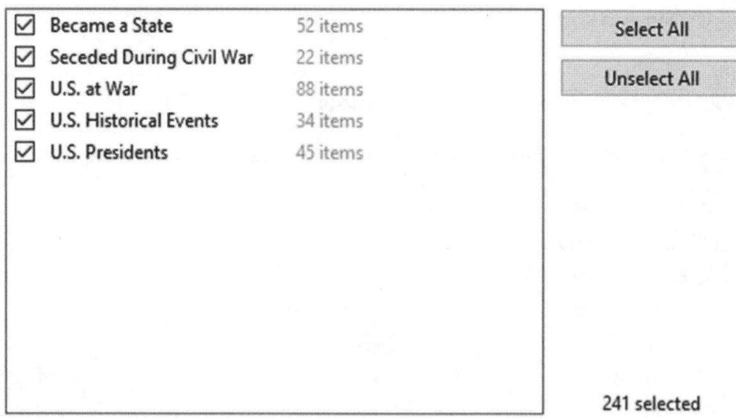
What types of items would you like to import?
Became a State 52 items
Seceded During Civil War 22 items
U.S. at War 88 items
U.S. Historical Events 34 items
U.S. Presidents 45 items
Select All
Unselect All
241 selected

Check the box next to each type of item you want and click **Next**.

▶ Choose Your Options

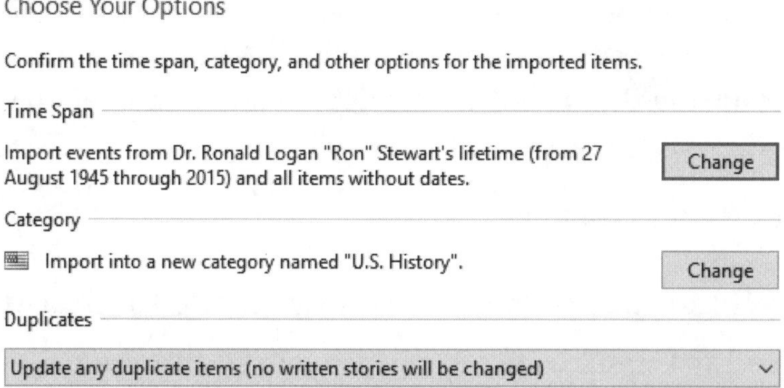
Choose Your Options
Confirm the time span, category, and other options for the imported items.
Time Span
Import events from Dr. Ronald Logan "Ron" Stewart's lifetime (from 27 August 1945 through 2015) and all items without dates.
Change
Category
Import into a new category named "U.S. History".
Change
Duplicates
Update any duplicate items (no written stories will be changed)

The last step is to adjust any options before importing the LifeCapsule.

> Time Span – click **Change** to change the time span of events imported. The default is only to include events from the subject's lifetime.

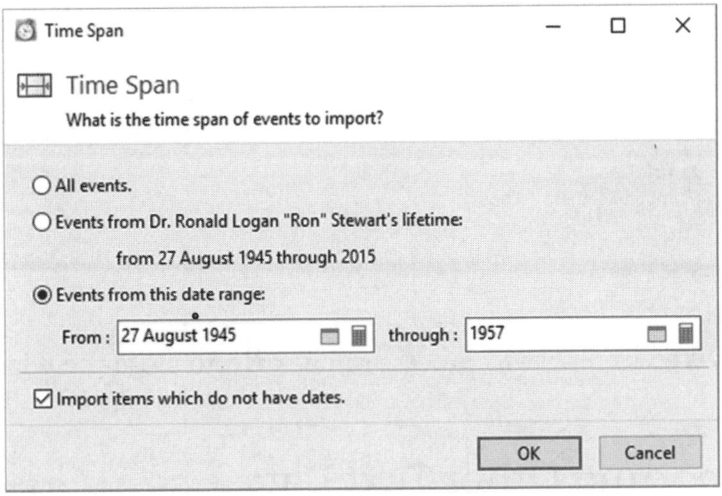

Time Span

Time Span

What is the time span of events to import?

All events.

Events from Dr. Ronald Logan "Ron" Stewart's lifetime:

from 27 August 1945 through 2015

Events from this date range:

From : 27 August 1945 through : 1957

Import items which do not have dates.

OK Cancel

You may want to adjust the time span when a LifeCapsule is only relevant to a specific period of the person's life.

For example, if you emigrated from England to the United States in 1957, you would want to import the "British History" LifeCapsule through 1957 and the "U.S. History" LifeCapsule from 1957 to the present.

Category – click **Change** to change the category of the imported stories. The default will be a category with the LifeCapsule's name.

Duplicates – select what you want to do with any duplicate stories: "Don't import any duplicate items", "Update any duplicate items (no written stories will be changed)", or "Import all duplicate items".

Click **Import** to begin the import.

▶ Would you like to import another LifeCapsule?

The final step asks you if you would like to import another LifeCapsule or not.

Would you like to import another LifeCapsule?

→ Yes
Import another LifeCapsule.

→ No
Close this wizard.

Click **Yes** to repeat to process or click **No** to close the wizard.

Importing Other Text Data

Some more tech-savvy users may have a need to import events to their Story List from a source besides their genealogy software or the LifeCapsules.

You can do this through a text file in either tab-delimited (.txt) or comma-separated (.csv) format. You'll want to start by arranging the data in a spreadsheet such as Microsoft Excel.

Use any combination of the following columns:

- **Title** – this is the "Title" of the story that will appear in the timeline/Story List.
- **Date** – this is the date of the story. While entering this into your spreadsheet, putting a single quote (') in front of the date will preserve your text.
- **Age** – the person's age at the time of the story.
- **Place** – the place where the story takes place.
- **Rating** – a rating (between 0 and 5) for the story.
- **Organizer Text** – text that will appear in the Organizer for the story.
- **Composer Text** – the main body of the story.

Be sure to put the names of the columns in the first row of the spreadsheet. It's recommended to use names as close to the previously mentioned column names as possible.

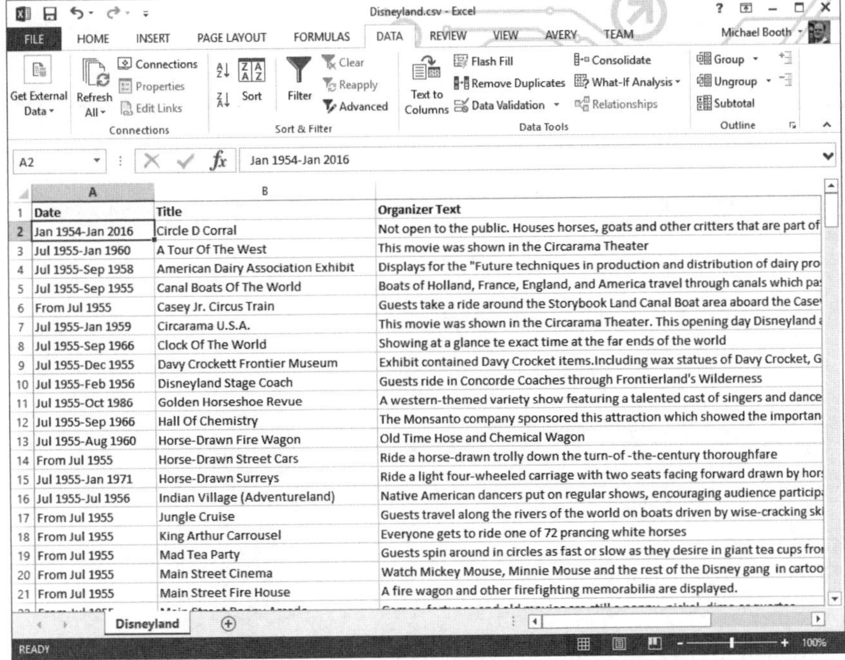

Once you have your spreadsheet ready, select **File** > **Save As** and give it a filename. Be sure to change the "File Type" to "Text (Tab Delimited)" or "CSV (Comma Delimited)". While the type that you choose isn't important, you'll need to remember your choice for a later step.

You can then import the text data into *Personal Historian* by selecting **File** > **Import** > **Import Text Data** from the Main Menu.

The "Import Text Data" wizard will appear.

▶ What is the format of the text data file?

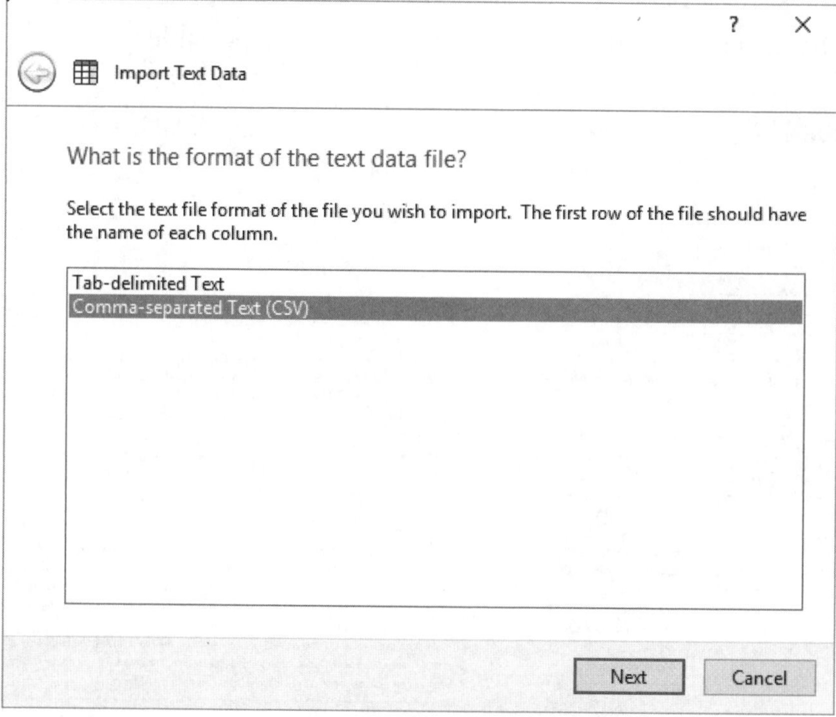

? ×
Import Text Data
What is the format of the text data file?
Select the text file format of the file you wish to import. The first row of the file should have the name of each column.
Tab-delimited Text
Comma-separated Text (CSV)
Next
Cancel

You must first select the type of text data file that you wish to import: Tab-delimited Text or Comma-separated Text (CSV).

Make your selection and click **Next**.

▶ Where is the file you wish to import?

The wizard now asks if you know where your text data file is.

Where is the file you wish to import?

→ I know where the file is
Let me browse my computer for the file.

→ I'm not sure where the file is
Search my computer for the file.

Click **I know where the file is** if you do. Click **I'm not sure where the file is** if you're not a cyborg and need the software to search your computer for your file.

▶ Which fields do you wish to import?

The next step will ask you to match up fields (columns) from the imported text data file and *Personal Historian*. The fields from your text data will appear in the list on the right. The available *Personal Historian* fields are on the left.

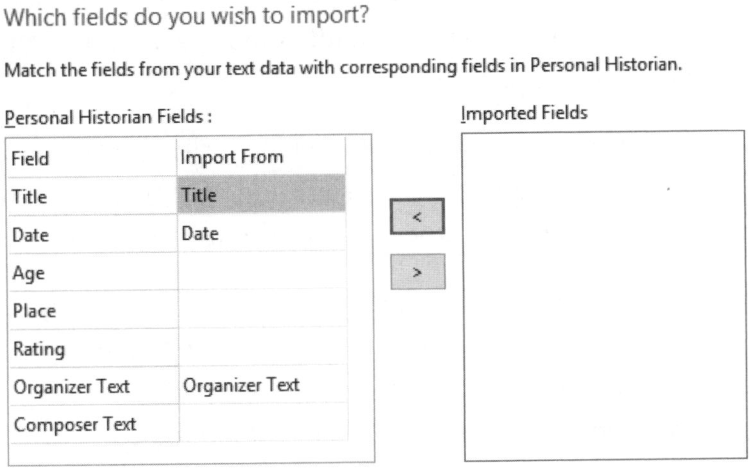

Which fields do you wish to import?

Match the fields from your text data with corresponding fields in Personal Historian.

Personal Historian Fields :

Field	Import From
Title	Title
Date	Date
Age	
Place	
Rating	
Organizer Text	Organizer Text
Composer Text	

< >

Imported Fields

The wizard will do its best to match up the fields for you by name. If there are any fields left in the "Imported Fields" list, select a field on each side and use the arrow buttons to match or unmatch the fields together.

Click **Next** to proceed.

▶ Choose Your Options

The last step is to adjust any options before importing the text data.

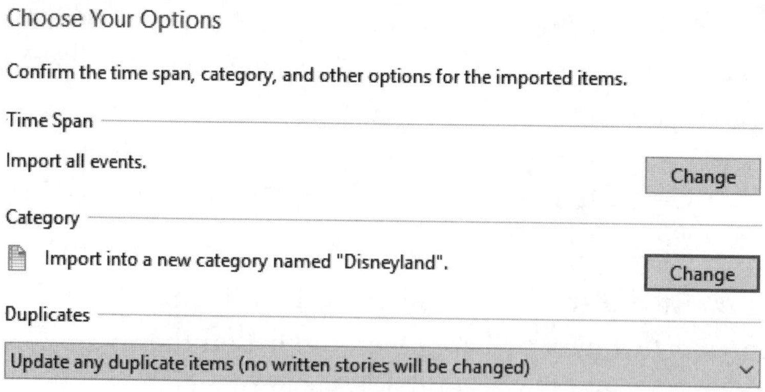

Choose Your Options

Confirm the time span, category, and other options for the imported items.

Time Span

Import all events. Change

Category

Import into a new category named "Disneyland". Change

Duplicates

Update any duplicate items (no written stories will be changed)

Time Span – click **Change** to change the time span of events imported. The default is only to include events from the subject's lifetime.

Category – click **Change** to change the category into which the imported events are added. The default will be a category with the name of the text data file.

Duplicates – select what you want to do with any duplicate stories: "Don't import any duplicate items", "Update any duplicate items (no written stories will be changed)", or "Import all duplicate items".

Click **Import** to begin the import and to close the wizard.

The Main Screen

The Main Screen is the heart of *Personal Historian*.

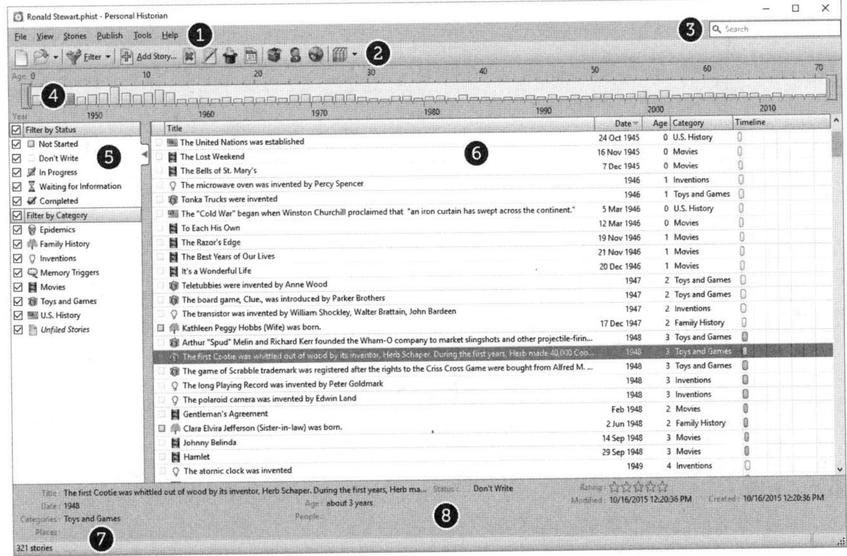

The Main Screen consists of:

1. Main Menu
2. Toolbar
3. Search Box
4. Time Slider
5. Sidebar
6. Story List
7. Status Bar
8. Story Details

Main Menu

File View Stories Publish Tools Help

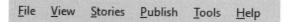

The Main Menu provides access to the many features of *Personal Historian*. Clicking on an item (like File, View, Stories, etc.) will cause a menu to drop down with more choices. Most options from the Main Menu are also available by clicking a button on the Toolbar or by using a shortcut key.

Toolbar

The Toolbar is a set of icons just above the Time Slider.

Each button performs a function that is available elsewhere, but it may be more convenient to use the buttons on the Toolbar. From left to right, the Toolbar buttons let you:

- Create a new file (see page 15)
- Open an existing file (see page 54)
- Filter the stories in the Story List (see page 47)
- Add a new story (see page 65)
- Edit the selected story (see page 65)
- Delete selected stories (see page 67)
- Edit a random story (see page 65)
- Add a journal story with today's date (see page 67)
- Edit categories (see page 69)
- Edit people (see page 75)
- Edit places (see page 81)
- Publish your personal history (see page 141)

Status Bar

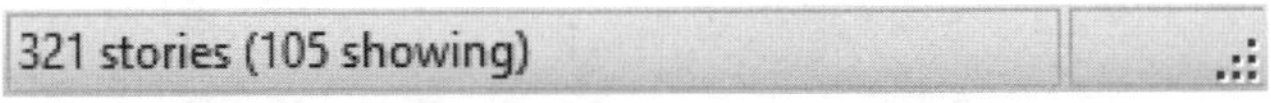

321 stories (105 showing)

The Status Bar on the Main Screen displays the number of stories in the file and, if a filter is applied, the number of stories that are currently displayed in the Story List.

Story Details

The Story Details, at the bottom of the Main Screen, displays information about the currently highlighted story.

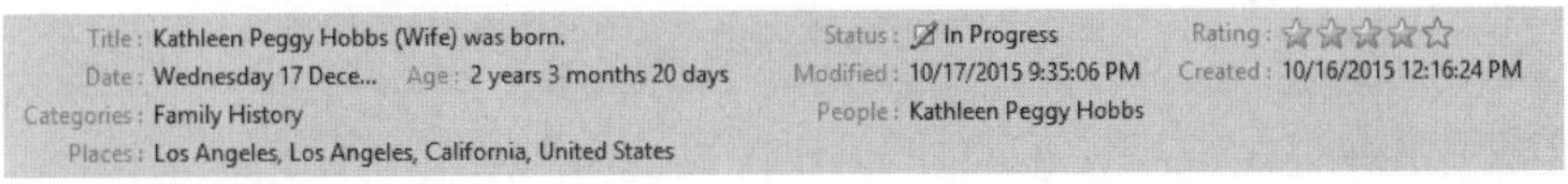

Title: Kathleen Peggy Hobbs (Wife) was born. Status: In Progress Rating:
Date: Wednesday 17 Dece... Age: 2 years 3 months 20 days Modified: 10/17/2015 9:35:06 PM Created: 10/16/2015 12:16:24 PM
Categories: Family History People: Kathleen Peggy Hobbs
Places: Los Angeles, Los Angeles, California, United States

The Story Details can be shown or hidden by selecting **View** > **Story Details** from the Main Menu.

Time Slider

The Time Slider extends across the width of the Main Screen. It gives you a visual overview of the person's life and shows you how much information you have. You can also see possible gaps in the history.

The Time Slider can be shown or hidden by selecting **View** > **Time Slider** from the Main Menu.

Along the top of the Time Slider is the individual's age. Along the bottom is the year. Each bar represents the number of stories in the overall file or if a filter is in place, the number of stories in the filter. The taller the bar, the more stories there are in the year. The shorter the bar, the fewer stories there are in the year.

Bars that have a darker color represent the years associated with the currently selected story in the Story List.

> *Personal Historian* will only show the Time Slider if the birth date of the individual has been set in the File Options. If you do not see the Time Slider on the Main Screen, go to the File Options and make sure that you have entered a birth date (or at least a birth year).

Let's look at an example. Here is the Time Slider of an individual who was born in 1955.

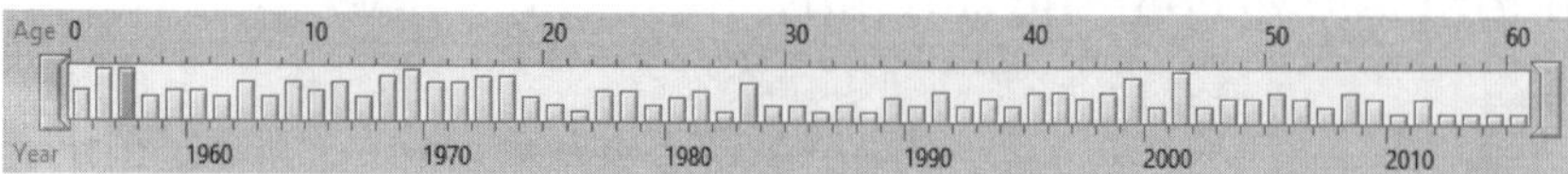

Each bar represents a year of this person's life. From the height of the bars, we can see that we have fewer stories between the ages of 20 and 40 and that we may want to concentrate on researching and writing about that particular time.

▶ Filtering Stories with the Time Slider

The Time Slider can be used to quickly filter the stories in the Story List to only include a specific range of years. On the left and right sides of the Time Slider are two bracket-shaped sliding bars. Using the mouse, slide these bars to filter the stories to only those years or ages within the brackets.

In the image above, all stories are visible. If you wanted to filter the stories to only include those stories between the age of 20 and 30 you can drag the sliders like this:

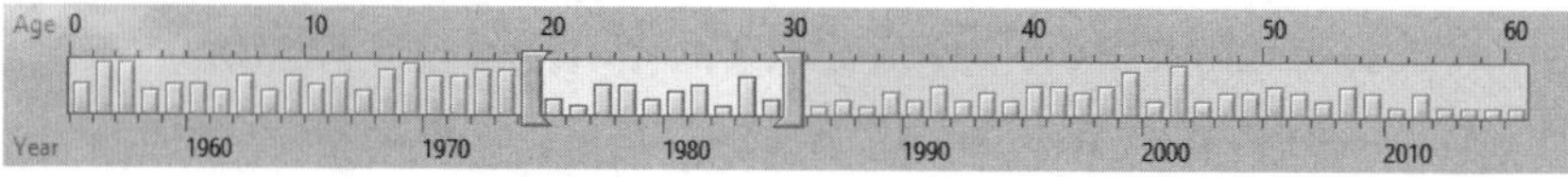

Story List

The Story List displays a list of all the stories in the file.

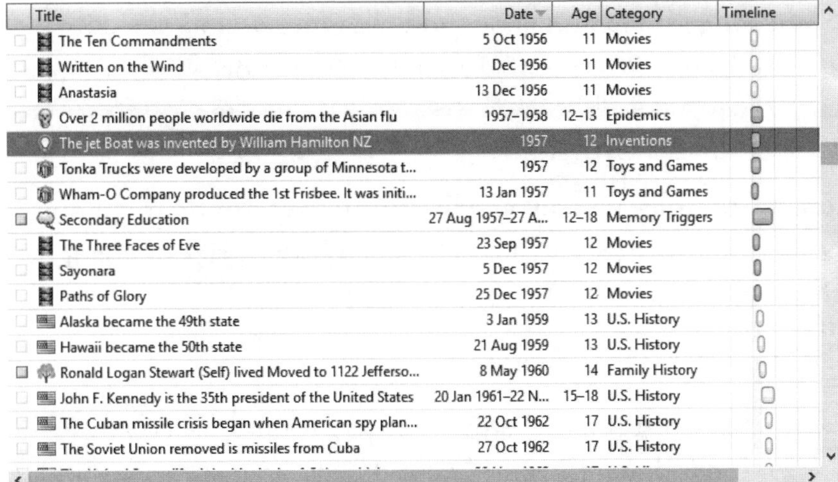

Title	Date	Age	Category	Timeline
The Ten Commandments	5 Oct 1956	11	Movies	
Written on the Wind	Dec 1956	11	Movies	
Anastasia	13 Dec 1956	11	Movies	
Over 2 million people worldwide die from the Asian flu	1957–1958	12–13	Epidemics	
The jet Boat was invented by William Hamilton NZ	1957	12	Inventions	
Tonka Trucks were developed by a group of Minnesota t...	1957	12	Toys and Games	
Wham-O Company produced the 1st Frisbee. It was initi...	13 Jan 1957	11	Toys and Games	
Secondary Education	27 Aug 1957–27 A...	12–18	Memory Triggers	
The Three Faces of Eve	23 Sep 1957	12	Movies	
Sayonara	5 Dec 1957	12	Movies	
Paths of Glory	25 Dec 1957	12	Movies	
Alaska became the 49th state	3 Jan 1959	13	U.S. History	
Hawaii became the 50th state	21 Aug 1959	13	U.S. History	
Ronald Logan Stewart (Self) lived Moved to 1122 Jefferso...	8 May 1960	14	Family History	
John F. Kennedy is the 35th president of the United States	20 Jan 1961–22 N...	15–18	U.S. History	
The Cuban missile crisis began when American spy plan...	22 Oct 1962	17	U.S. History	
The Soviet Union removed is missiles from Cuba	27 Oct 1962	17	U.S. History	

Each column of the Story List represents a different piece of information about the stories. Possible columns include:

- **Status** - the status (in progress, completed, etc.)
- **Title** - the title of the story
- **Date** - the date or time period for the story
- **Age** - the age of the person in the story
- **Category** - the categories to which you have assigned the story
- **Place** - the place (or places) associated with the story
- **People** - the person (or people) associated with the story
- **Rating** - your rating (from 0-5 stars) for the story
- **Date Modified** - the date the story was last worked on
- **Date Created** - the date the story was created
- **Timeline** - a graphical timeline showing when that particular story occurred during the person's life

Filters can be applied to the Story List to reduce the number of stories displayed and make the personal history easier to manage.

For more information about adding, editing, and deleting stories from the list, see "Managing Your Stories" on page 63.

▶ Selecting Stories

There are times when you will want to select more than one story from the Story List (such as deleting stories or changing the status or category).

To select more than one story:

1. Click on the first story that you want to select.
2. Hold down the **Ctrl** key and click on all of the other stories that you want to select.
3. Each story that you click on will be selected.

To select a continuous block of stories:

1. Click on the top-most story that you want to select.
2. Hold down the **Shift** key and click on the bottom-most story that you want to select.
3. All stories from the top-most story to the bottom-most story will be selected.

You can also combine the **Ctrl** and **Shift** keys to select multiple continuous blocks of stories.

▶ Sorting Stories

When writing and publishing your story, you will often want to sort the stories in the Story List by date, title, age, category, status, date created, or date last modified.

To sort the stories in the Story List:

1. From the Main Menu, select **View** > **List Layout**. The "Story List Layout" screen will appear.
2. Click the **Sorting** tab.

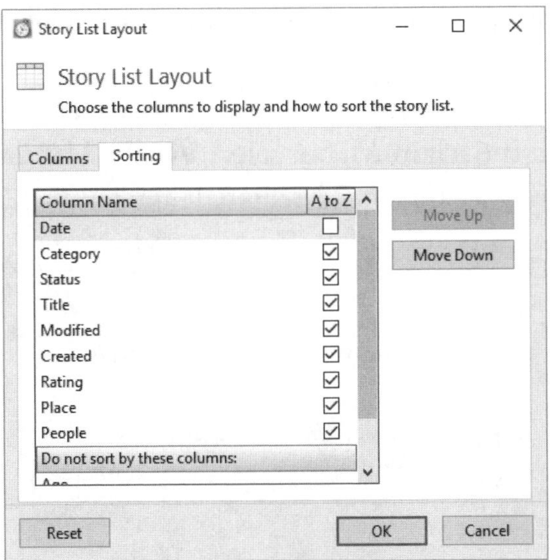

3. Use the **Move Up** and **Move Down** buttons to change the order of columns to sort by.
4. Check the **A to Z** checkbox to sort in ascending order. Uncheck it to sort the columns in descending order.

You can also sort the Story List by clicking on the top of the column you wish to sort by. If you click the column a second time, it will reverse the direction of the sort.

> Categories are sorted by their designated order, not alphabetically. By changing the order of the categories, you can affect the way that they are sorted. (See page 74)

▶ Choosing Which Columns to Display

When working with stories, you may decide that you want to see fewer or more columns of information. You can tell *Personal Historian* exactly which columns to display.

To choose which columns to display in the Story List:

1. From the Main Menu, select **View** > **List Layout**. The "Story List Layout" screen will appear.

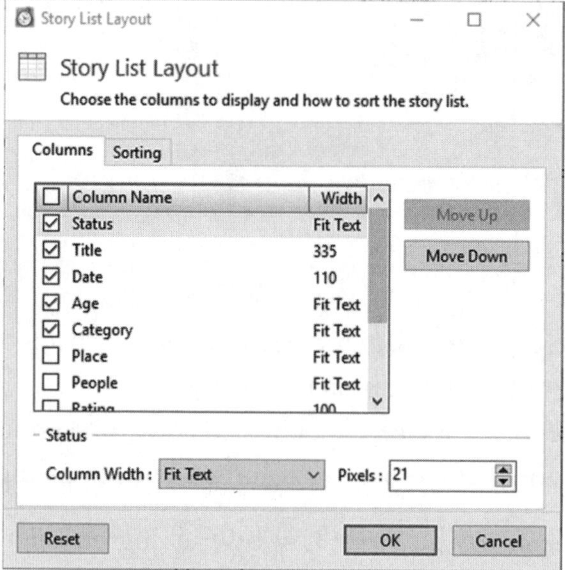

2. Select the name of the column that you wish to show or hide (a checkmark will indicate if the column is currently visible).
3. Use the **Column Width** box to change the size of the column.

You can also access the list of columns by right-clicking on the header of the Story List.

▶ Resizing the Columns

You may occasionally need to change the width of a column in order to make room for other columns or to see some text which is hidden.

To resize a column in the Story List:

1. On the Story List's header, use the mouse to drag the line to the right of the column that you wish to resize.
2. When the column is the desired width, release the mouse button.

▶ Changing the Order of the Columns

By default, the columns in the Story List are in the following order: Story Status, Title, Date, Age, Category, Date Last Modified, and Date Created. However, you may wish to change the order of these columns to one that better suits your thinking style.

To change the order of a column in the Story List:

1. On the Story List's header, use the mouse to drag the column's title from its original position.
2. When the column is at its desired position in the Story List, release the mouse button.

Search Box

Personal Historian includes a powerful full-text search of all the stories in your file. Just type the text you are searching for into the Search Box located in the upper-right corner of the Main Screen.

Personal Historian will filter your Story List based on what you type into that box. For example, if you typed the word **`James`** into the Search Box, *Personal Historian* might filter your Story List like this:

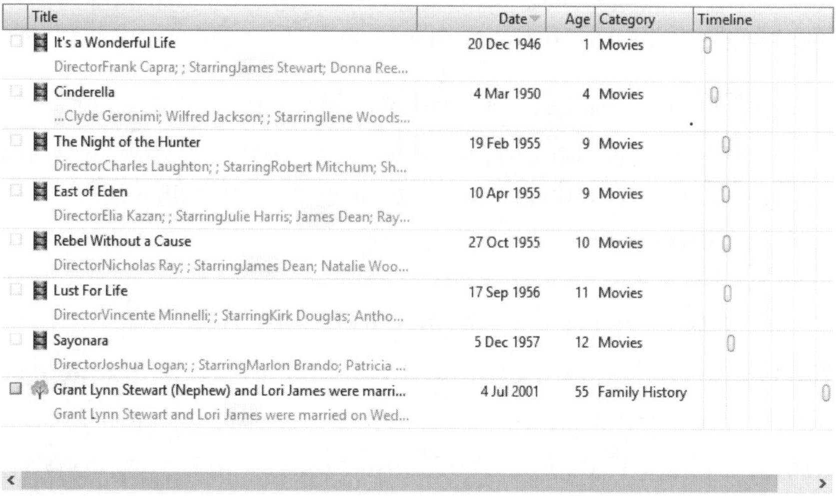

Title	Date	Age	Category	Timeline
It's a Wonderful Life DirectorFrank Capra; ; StarringJames Stewart; Donna Ree...	20 Dec 1946	1	Movies	
Cinderella ...Clyde Geronimi; Wilfred Jackson; ; StarringIlene Woods...	4 Mar 1950	4	Movies	
The Night of the Hunter DirectorCharles Laughton; ; StarringRobert Mitchum; Sh...	19 Feb 1955	9	Movies	
East of Eden DirectorElia Kazan; ; StarringJulie Harris; James Dean; Ray...	10 Apr 1955	9	Movies	
Rebel Without a Cause DirectorNicholas Ray; ; StarringJames Dean; Natalie Woo...	27 Oct 1955	10	Movies	
Lust For Life DirectorVincente Minnelli; ; StarringKirk Douglas; Antho...	17 Sep 1956	11	Movies	
Sayonara DirectorJoshua Logan; ; StarringMarlon Brando; Patricia ...	5 Dec 1957	12	Movies	
Grant Lynn Stewart (Nephew) and Lori James were marri... Grant Lynn Stewart and Lori James were married on Wed...	4 Jul 2001	55	Family History	

But the full-text search is much more powerful than just finding stories with a particular word.

- **Finding a group of words** - Just type in the words. Typing **`James Utah`** will select stories which have both James and Utah somewhere in them. You can also put the word **`AND`** between the words you are looking for (like **`James AND Utah`**) but that isn't required.
- **Finding any words** - If you type words with **`OR`** between them, it will select stories which have one or the other (or both) words. Typing **`James OR Utah`** will select stories with either **`James`** or **`Utah`** in it (or both).
- **Finding a phrase** - Put double quotes around the phrase. Typing **`"James Utah"`** will select stories

with that exact phrase, but not if the two words are separated in the story.

- **Finding part of a word** - You can use the asterisk as a wildcard. Typing `Jame*` will select stories with James, Jamestown, or any other word starting with "Jame".
- **Finding missing words** - If you enter a minus sign **-** in front of a word, it will select stories that don't have that word. Typing `-James` will select stories without the word James in it.

You can also mix and match any of these rules to create very powerful search results for your stories. If you entered `James OR -Smith*`, you will get a list of stories that either have the word "James" or which don't have any word starting with "Smith".

Filtering Stories

It is not uncommon to have hundreds of stories in a file, especially after importing genealogical data (see page 21) and LifeCapsules (see page 27). While all of the information may be useful and will eventually be useful in your writing, it can be overwhelming to look at; especially when it isn't needed at the moment.

This is where filtering comes in. Filters allow you to look at only relevant stories. The stories aren't removed from the file; they are only temporarily hidden.

Let's take an example. Imagine you are interested in seeing stories about your father's teenage years. You know that he was a teenager between 1921 and 1929. You set a date filter for all of the stories that occurred between 1921 and 1929.

Suddenly the number of stories in the Story List is greatly reduced. If you want to narrow it down even more, you may decide that you don't need to see stories from the "U.S. Holidays" category. You change the Categories filter, indicating that you don't want to see anything from the "U.S. Holidays" category. The Story List has fewer stories now. Suddenly, the overwhelming task becomes manageable.

Personal Historian has four different ways to filter stories:

1. **Sidebar** - quickly filter by story status and category
2. **Filter Screen** - complete control over all filtering options
3. **Time Slider** - filter by year (see page 39)
4. **Search Box** – filter by text within the title and story itself (see page 45).

▶ Sidebar

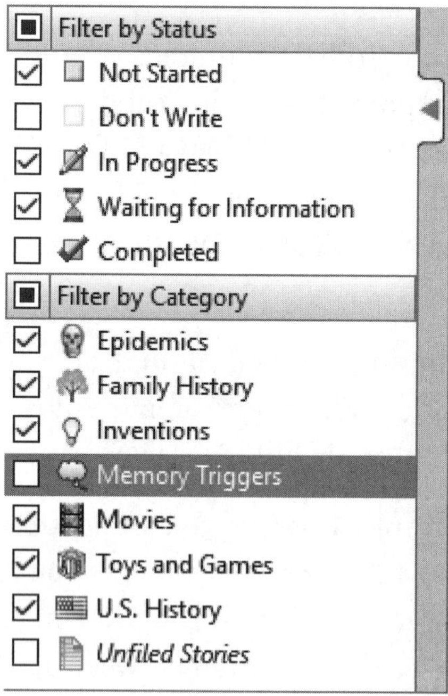

The Sidebar lets you quickly filter out stories based on their status or category. If a story status or category in the panel is checked, stories with that status or category will be displayed. If an item is unchecked, *Personal Historian* will hide stories with that status or category.

The Time Slider can be shown or hidden by selecting **View** > **Sidebar** from the Main Menu.

You may also click on the box next to "Filter by Status" or "Filter by Category" to check or uncheck all the items at once.

You can resize the Sidebar by moving the mouse just to the right of the panel, holding down the left mouse button, and dragging it to the left or right.

Click on the small arrow in the area to quickly hide or show the Sidebar.

▶ Filter Screen

To open the Filter Screen, select **View** > **Filter** from the Main Menu, or click the Filter button on the Toolbar.

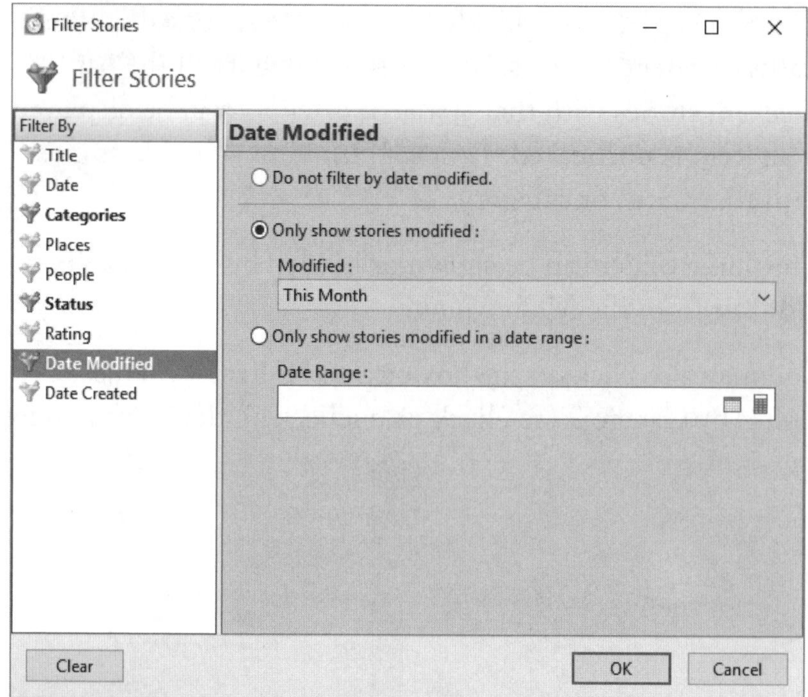

You can filter by a story's Title, Date, Categories, Places, People, Status, Rating, Date Modified, or Date Created.

▶ Removing a Filter

To remove the filter from the Story List, select **View** > **Remove Filter** from the Main Menu.

▶ Saving and Reusing Filters

Personal Historian lets you save filters that you have created, so that you can select and use them again later.

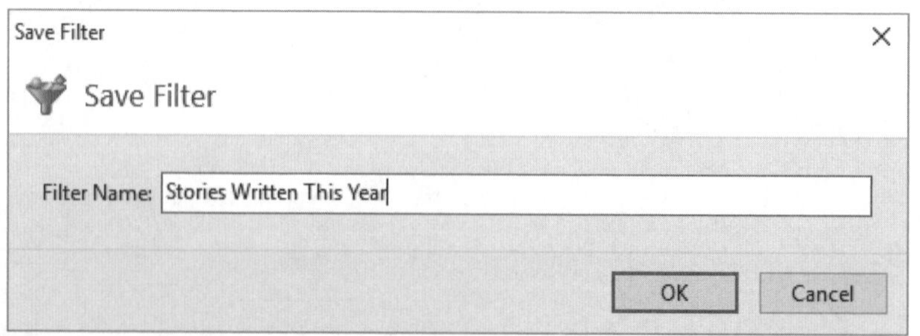

Once you have a filter you like, select **View** > **Saved Filters** > **Save Filter** from the Main Menu, and enter a name for the current filter (something that describes the filter settings).

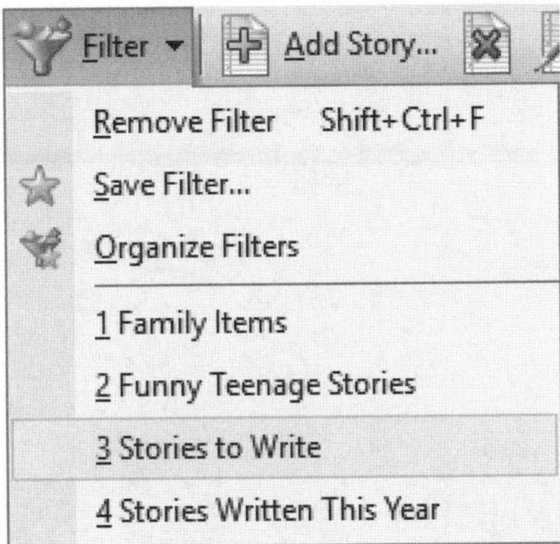

You can then reuse that filter later by doing **View** > **Saved Filters** from the menu and selecting a filter by name.

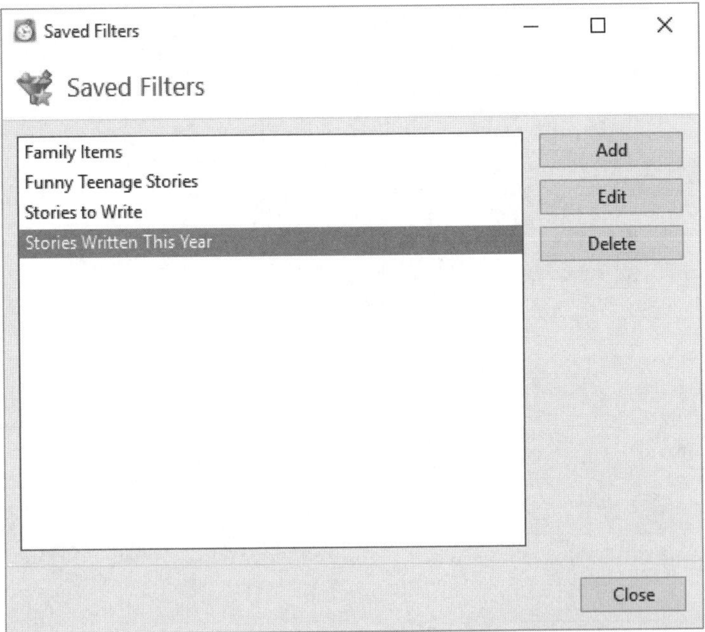

To add, edit, or delete Saved Filters, choose **View** > **Organize Filters** from the Main Menu.

Working with Files

You can use *Personal Historian* to write an unlimited number of histories. You simply create a new file for each person or group.

Taming and organizing those files can sometimes be challenging. But with a little bit of care and with help from *Personal Historian*, you can keep those files in line.

> *Personal Historian* keeps all of a person's history in a single file that ends with the letters ".phist". This file includes all the data, stories, and even pictures that you've added to the history.

By default, the files are kept in the "Data Files" folder that you set up in the Program Options (see page 167). If you don't specify a Data Files folder, *Personal Historian* will expect them to be in your Documents folder.

Of course, you always have the option of using files in any drive or folder besides the default. But keeping your files in a single location can help you avoid misplaced files, multiple copies of files, and general confusion.

Open an Existing File

To open an existing file:

1. From the Main Menu, select **File** > **Open** or click the "Open File" button on the Toolbar.
2. A screen will appear prompting you for the name of the *Personal Historian* file. Type in the filename, taking care that you are in the correct disk drive and folder.
3. Click the **Open** button.

If you click on the small arrow to the right of the "Open File" Toolbar button or select **File** > **Open Recent** from the Main Menu, you will see a list of your most recently used files. Click a filename to open that file.

Searching for a File

Sometimes, despite your best efforts, you may not be able to remember where a file is located. *Personal Historian* can search your computer and show you a list of all the files that it finds.

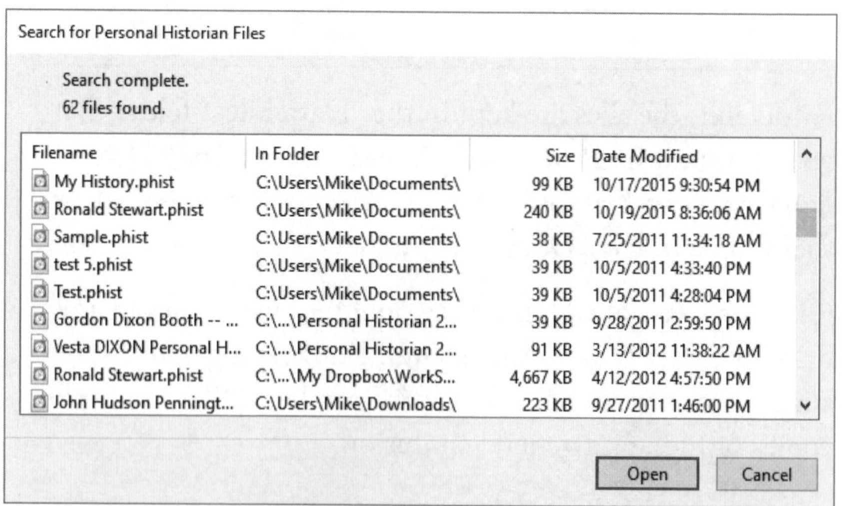

To search for files, select **File** > **Search for Files** from the Main Menu.

A screen will appear showing the filename, location, size, and date of each personal history file as it is found. Click on the desired filename and then the **Open** button.

Moving or Renaming a File

If you need to move a file to a different folder or give it a different filename, select **File** > **Rename** from the Main Menu.

A screen will appear prompting you for the file's new location and name. Type in the new filename, taking care that you are in the disk drive and folder where you wish the put the file. Click the **Save** button to complete the change.

Deleting a File

To delete an existing file, select **File** > **Delete** from the Main Menu.

> This is **not** deleting a single story. This is deleting the **entire file** including all of its stories, pictures, and other data about the person.
>
> Only do this if you are certain you have a better copy of the file someplace else or if the subject of the history ran over your cat.

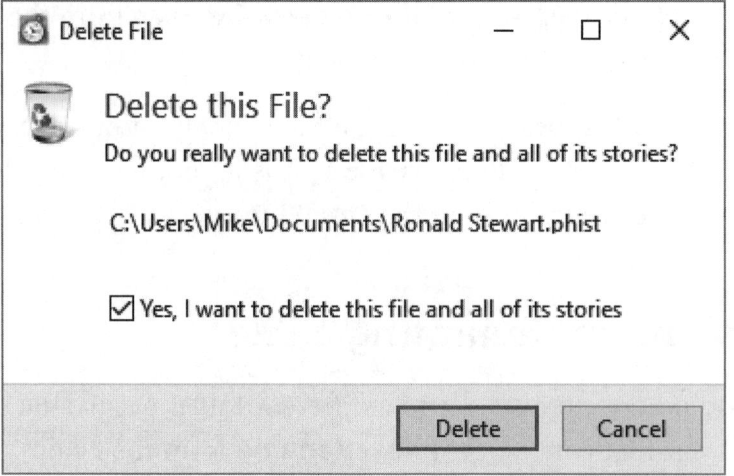

A message will appear asking you to confirm the deletion. You must check the box labeled **Yes** and click **Delete**.

> If you get "deleter's remorse", there may still be hope. The file is sent to your computer's Recycle Bin and may still be recoverable. Do an internet search for "undelete from recycle bin" for instructions.

Copying a File

To make a copy an existing file, select **File** > **Copy**. A message will appear prompting you for the new filename.

Type in the name you wish to give the file, taking care that you are in the correct disk drive and folder where you wish the file to reside. Click the **Save** button to create the copy.

Making a copy of a file has its uses but should be done with care. By having multiple copies of the same history, you may make changes to the original file and then accidentally make different changes to the copy. Reconciling the files would be difficult and time-consuming.

Making multiple copies of a file is like naming all of your kids, "Dave." It's unnecessary and just makes it more difficult to keep track of which one you asked to mow the lawn, which one you asked to take out the trash, or which one borrowed $10 to go to the movies.

> If you are copying a file as a way of backing up your data, make an actual backup instead (see page 159). It's cleaner and more effective than making a straight copy of the file.

Checking and Repairing a File

If you're curious about how much information is in your file, select **File** > **Properties** from the Main Menu.

You'll see a screen that will show you the file's location, name, size, date created, and date last modified.

You'll also see the number of stories, categories, people, and places you have in your file.

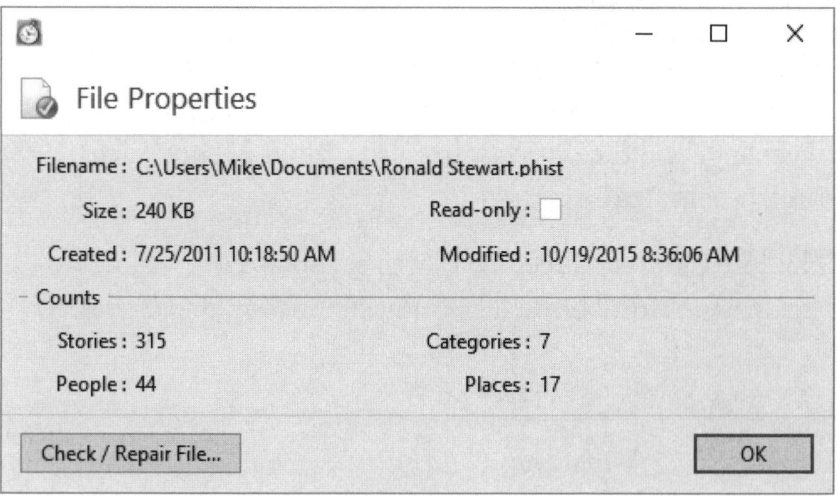

If you haven't yet noticed, computers and software aren't perfect. Sometimes data gets corrupted for any number of reasons. That's why it's always important to keep backups of your data (see page 159).

Personal Historian can check and often even repair a damaged file. If you suspect that your file may have some corruption, click **Check / Repair File** on the File Properties screen.

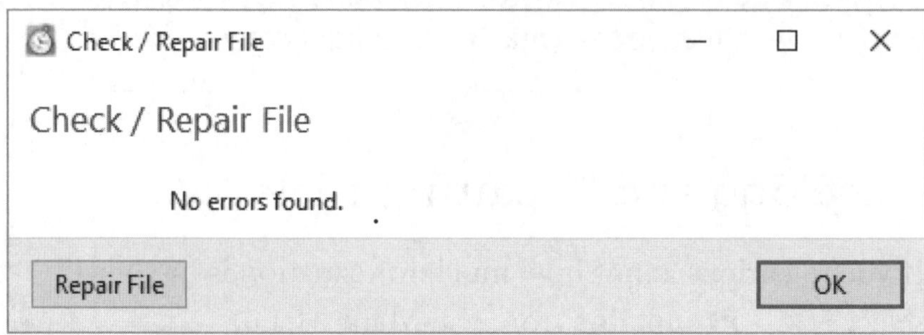

Personal Historian will test the file and look for any problems. If it finds any, click **Repair File** to attempt to fix the problems.

File Options

Each file has a set of options to tell *Personal Historian* details about the subject person, author, or styles to use for that file. To change the file options, from the Main Menu, select **Tools** > **File Options**.

The File Options screen has three sections, each visible by clicking the icon on the left: Subject, Author, and Styles.

▶ Subject

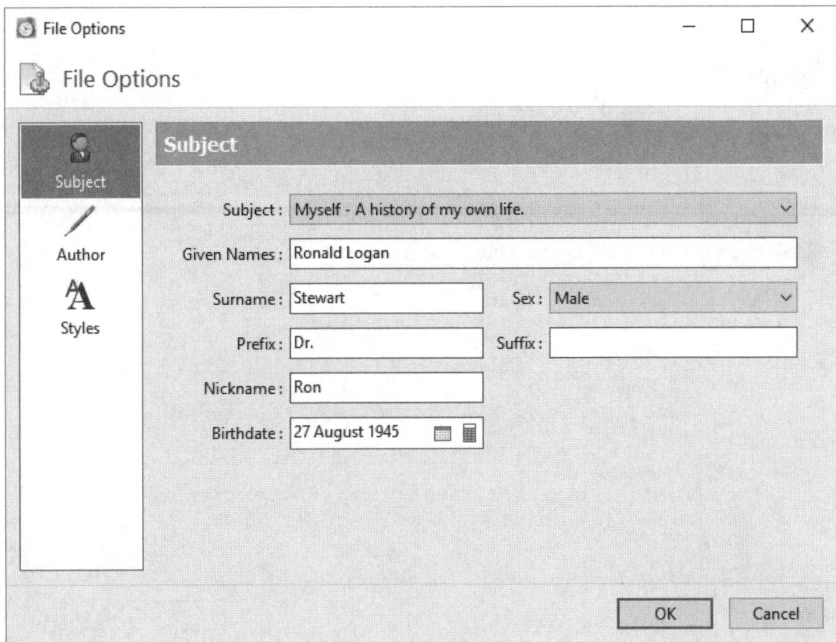

The Subject section lets you enter information about the person or group that the file is about.

You can choose what type of subject (yourself, another person, or a group), and then enter information about that subject.

▶ Author

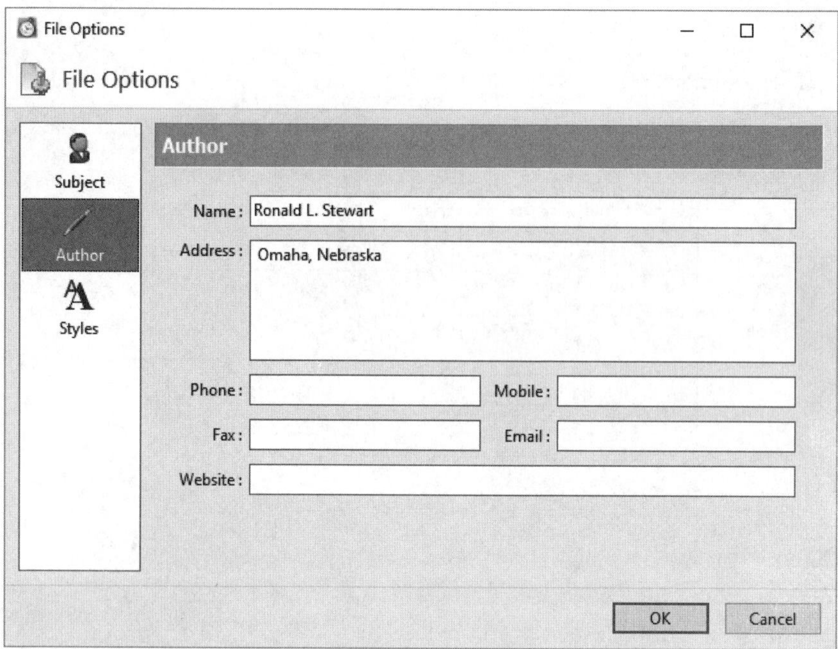

The Author option lets you enter information about yourself (the person writing the personal history). You can enter your name, address, phone numbers, email address, or a personal website address.

The information about the author is used when publishing a book (see page 141) and used to fill out information on the cover, title pages, and elsewhere.

▶ Styles

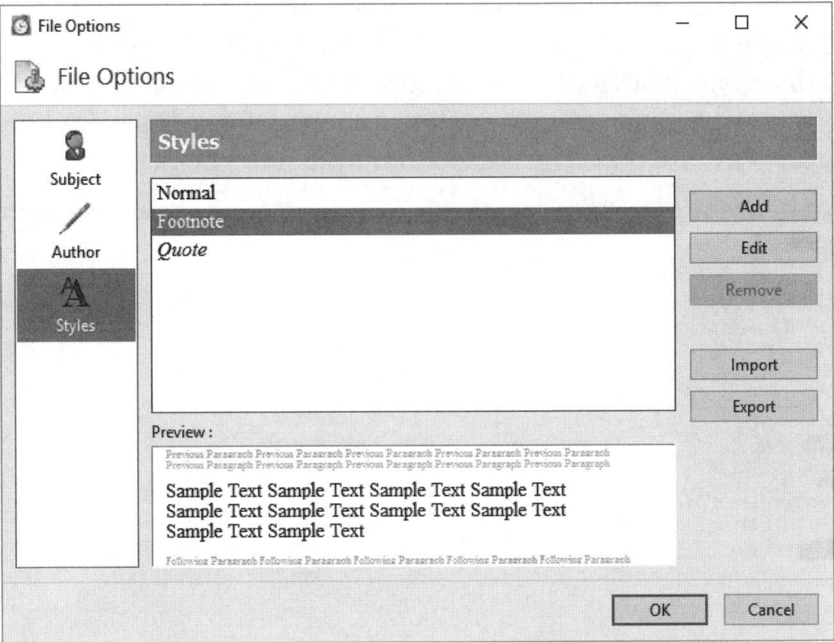

The Styles option lets you create "styles" that you can use as you write the stories in your personal history. A style is a combination of a typeface (Arial, Times Roman, etc.), a font size, font characteristics (bold, italics, color, etc.), paragraph settings (indent, spacing, and alignment).

You can create a new style by clicking the **Add** button, change an existing style by highlighting the style in the list and clicking **Edit**, or delete a style by clicking the **Remove** button.

If you have styles that you like, the **Export** will save the styles to a file. Open a different *Personal Historian* file and use the **Import** button to load the styles from the exported file so that you don't have to recreate them.

When you are typing a story, you can change the style for any paragraph by selecting the style from a list. It's better to use styles than to directly set text fonts and sizes. Changing the appearance of a style will also change the appearance everywhere that style is used throughout the book.

Managing Your Stories

A story is the basic unit of a personal history file. By dividing a history into smaller, individual stories, it becomes easier to remember, organize, and write a history. There is no practical limit to the number of stories that a personal history can contain.

A story includes a title, category, and status and may also include a date, age, text, and pictures. It may also reference any number of people or places.

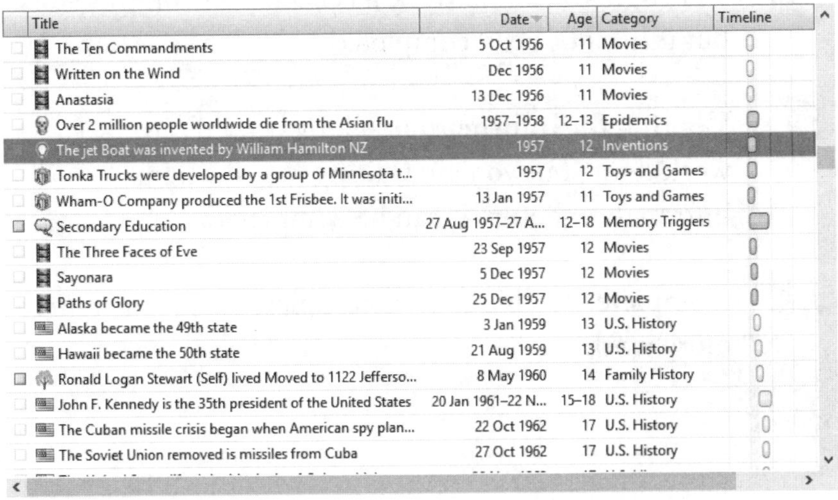

Title	Date	Age	Category	Timeline
The Ten Commandments	5 Oct 1956	11	Movies	
Written on the Wind	Dec 1956	11	Movies	
Anastasia	13 Dec 1956	11	Movies	
Over 2 million people worldwide die from the Asian flu	1957–1958	12–13	Epidemics	
The jet Boat was invented by William Hamilton NZ	1957	12	Inventions	
Tonka Trucks were developed by a group of Minnesota t...	1957	12	Toys and Games	
Wham-O Company produced the 1st Frisbee. It was initi...	13 Jan 1957	11	Toys and Games	
Secondary Education	27 Aug 1957–27 A...	12–18	Memory Triggers	
The Three Faces of Eve	23 Sep 1957	12	Movies	
Sayonara	5 Dec 1957	12	Movies	
Paths of Glory	25 Dec 1957	12	Movies	
Alaska became the 49th state	3 Jan 1959	13	U.S. History	
Hawaii became the 50th state	21 Aug 1959	13	U.S. History	
Ronald Logan Stewart (Self) lived Moved to 1122 Jefferso...	8 May 1960	14	Family History	
John F. Kennedy is the 35th president of the United States	20 Jan 1961–22 N...	15–18	U.S. History	
The Cuban missile crisis began when American spy plan...	22 Oct 1962	17	U.S. History	
The Soviet Union removed is missiles from Cuba	27 Oct 1962	17	U.S. History	

The Main Screen displays stories in the Story List (see page 41). The Story List can be filtered, sorted, and customized to your needs.

Story Status

Every story is assigned a status to show its progress. A story's status helps you keep track of your work and assists you in sorting, filtering, and finding stories that need work.

The status is represented visually by an icon in the Story List and can easily be changed on the Editor Screen (see page 87). The possible status values are:

- **Not Started** - No work has begun on this story.
- **Don't Write** – This story will not be written. It is in the Story List merely for context or as a reminder.
- **In Progress** - Some work has been done on this story but it has not been completed.
- **Waiting for Information** – This story has some work done, but you are waiting for additional information before it can be completed.
- **Completed** - This story is complete and requires no more work.

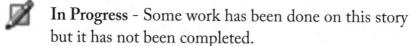

Adding a New Story

While some of your stories possibly came from your genealogy or LifeCapsules (see page 27), much of the history will consist of stories that you add yourself.

Add Story... Add a new story by selecting **Stories** > **Add Story** from the Main Menu, by clicking the "Add Story" button on the Toolbar, or by pressing **Shift** + **Enter** on your keyboard.

A blank Editor Screen (see page 87) will appear where you can write the new story.

Editing an Existing Story

Change or write about an existing story by first selecting it in the Story List. Then choose **Stories** > **Edit Story** from the Main Menu, click the "Edit Story" Toolbar button, press **Ctrl** + **Enter** on your keyboard, or double-click the story with your mouse.

The Editor Screen (see page 87) will appear with the story-ready to edit or update.

Picking a Random Story

This button is my wife's favorite. Sometimes, you just can't make up your mind what you want to write about on a given day.

If you've hit a memory block, *Personal Historian* can pick a random story from the Story List for you. This can be useful if you can't decide what to work on next or if you are feeling overwhelmed. It will only pick a story if its status is "Not Started."

To pick a random story, choose **Stories** > **Edit Random Story** from the Main Menu, click the "Random Story" Toolbar button, or press **Alt** + **Enter** on your keyboard. The "Pick a Random Story" screen will appear.

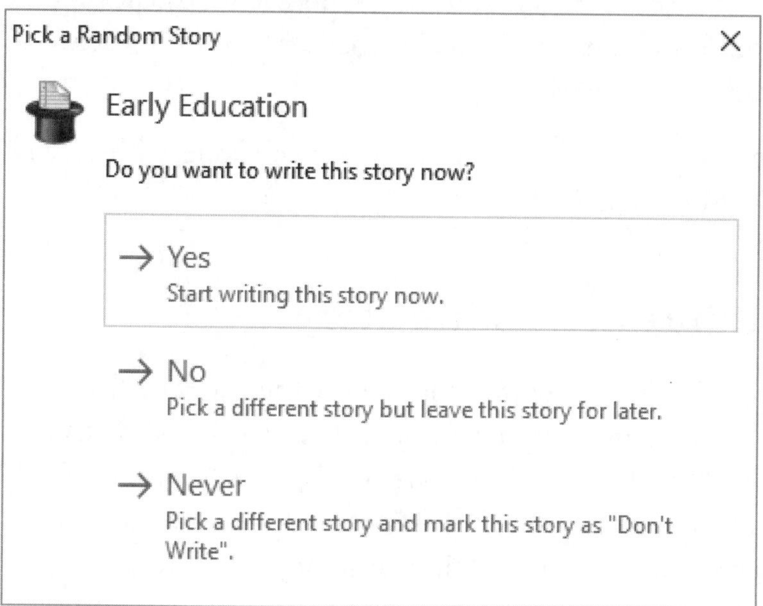

Click **Yes** to start writing this story now, **No** to pick a different story but leave this story for later, or **Never** to pick a different story and change the status of this one as, "Don't Write."

Another benefit to working on a random story is to stimulate memories from a different perspective. If you've been spending a lot of time writing about a particular subject or time period, your thoughts can get stuck in ruts, making it difficult to remember details or continue in your train of thought.

Working on a completely random story can often push you past your memory block. After you've written about the random topic, you may return to the original story and find that your writing can again continue.

Adding a Journal Entry

Personal Historian is also useful for keeping a day-to-day journal. Adding a journal entry is simply adding a new story with today's date already entered.

To add a journal entry select **Stories** > **Add Journal Entry**, click the "Journal Entry" Toolbar button, or press **Ctrl** + **J** on your keyboard.

The Editor Screen (see page 87) will appear with a new entry with the current date already entered.

Deleting a Story

To permanently delete one or more stories from the Story List, select the story(s) that you wish to delete (see "Selecting Stories" on page 42).

Select **Stories** > **Delete Stories**, click the "Delete Stories" Toolbar button, or press **Ctrl** + **Delete** on your keyboard.

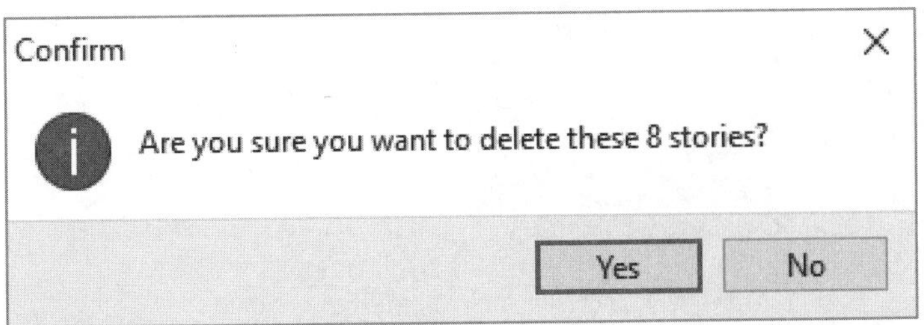

When asked to confirm the deletion, click **Yes** to delete the stories.

Using Categories

Categories help organize the stories of a personal history into similar groups and assist the user in sorting, filtering, and finding stories. Each story may belong to multiple categories. If a story does not have a category, it is labeled "Unfiled".

Each category can have a unique icon, font style, and color to make its stories easily recognizable in the Main Screen.

There is no practical limit to the number of categories that a file can contain. Users are encouraged to create categories that complement their writing and thinking styles.

When it comes time to publish the history (see page 141), you have the option of using the categories to create the chapters in the book.

To bring up the list of categories in your personal history, select **Stories > Categories** from the Main Menu or click the "Categories" button on the Toolbar.

A list of all categories in the file will appear.

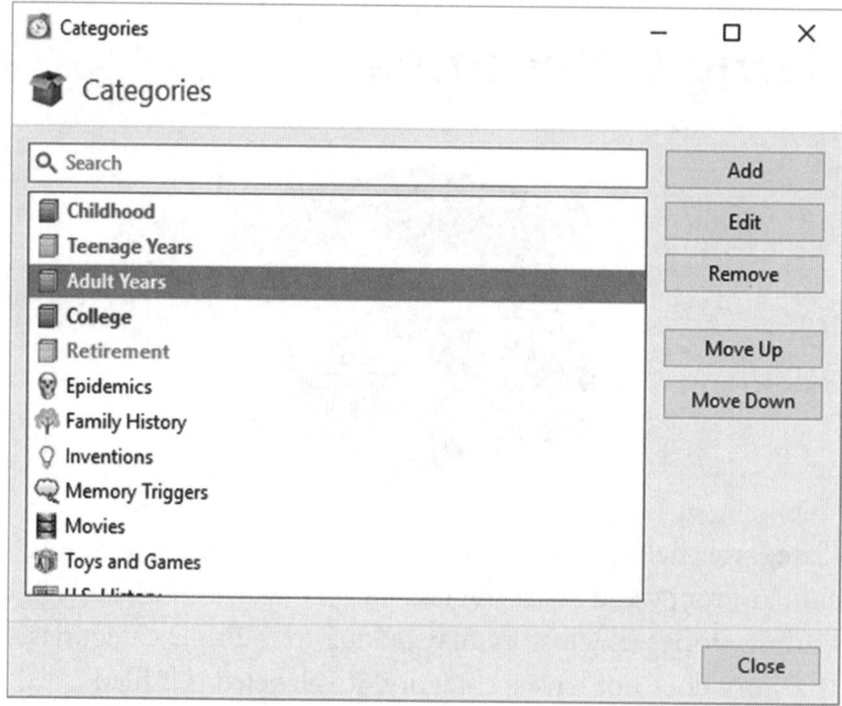

From this screen, you can add, edit, remove, and rearrange the categories in the file.

Adding a New Category

To add a new category to the file, click the **Add** button to bring up the "Add Category" screen.

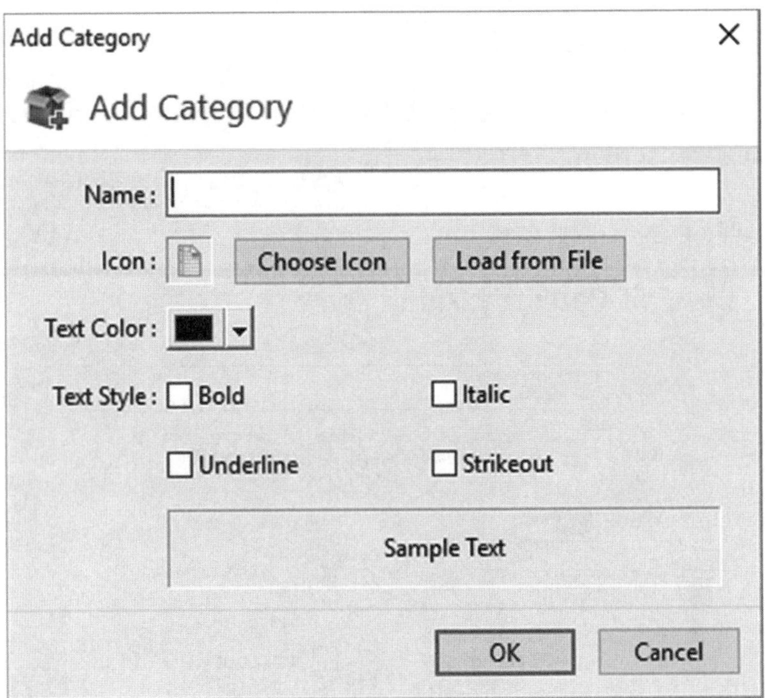

You can enter the name for the new category, as well as select an icon, text color and style for the category.

> By changing the icon, text color and style, you can make stories stand out on the main Story List based on their category.

Click **Choose Icon** to see a list of built-in icons that you can assign to the category. Click **Load from File** to select a picture file from your computer to use as the icon.

Editing a Category

To edit a category, click the **Edit** button to bring up the "Edit Category" screen.

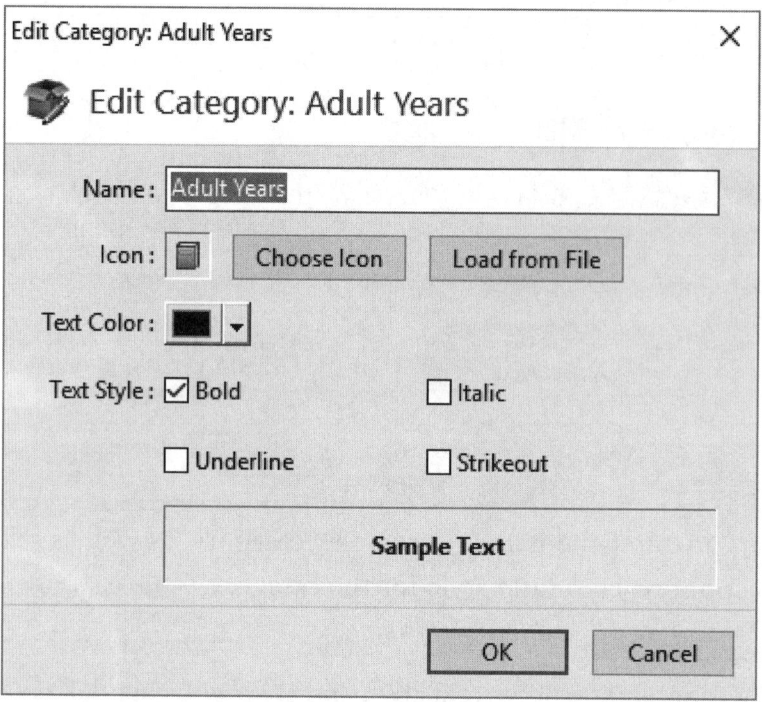

Here, you can edit the category information on the same screen that you originally added the category. You can rename the category or change the icon, text color, or text style for the category.

Deleting a Category

To remove a category, click the **Remove** button.

If there are no stories that are using the category, you will be asked to confirm the deletion.

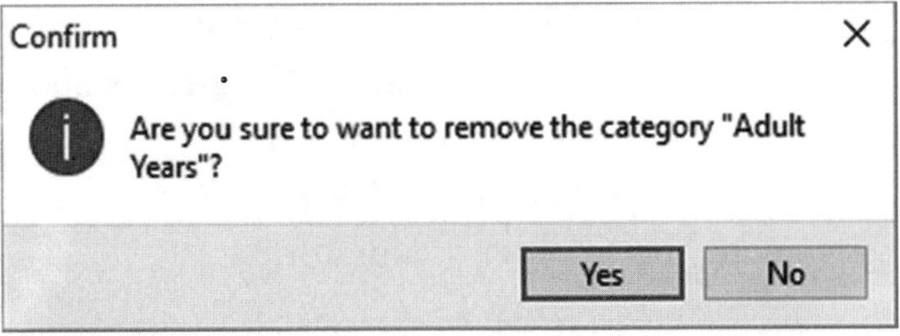

If there are stories assigned to the category you want to delete, *Personal Historian* lets you choose what to do with those stories.

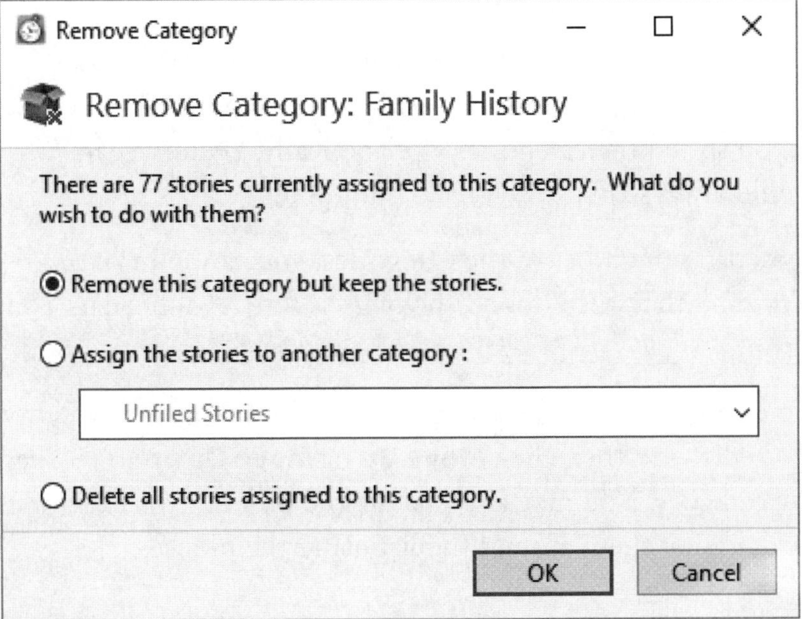

Remove Category
Remove Category: Family History
There are 77 stories currently assigned to this category. What do you wish to do with them?
Remove this category but keep the stories.
Assign the stories to another category :
Unfiled Stories
Delete all stories assigned to this category.
OK
Cancel

You have four options:

1. **Remove this category but keep the stories** – this will delete the category and mark all of its stories as "Unfiled".
2. **Assign the stories to another category** – this will delete the category and assign its stories to the category chosen from the box.

3. **Delete all stories assigned to this category** – the nuclear option. This will delete the category and its stories. This cannot be undone.
4. **Cancel** – this returns to the last screen without removing the category or any stories.

Changing the Order of Categories

Categories are **not** sorted alphabetically in the Story List. They are sorted by an order that you designate.

For example, say you have categories entitled "Childhood," "Teenage Years," "College," "Adult Years," and "Retirement." If you sorted the categories alphabetically, "Adult Years" would always appear before "Childhood."

By setting the order of the categories, you can tell *Personal Historian* that "Childhood" belongs before "Adult Years", and so on.

To change the order of the categories, highlight the category in the list and then click **Move Up** or **Move Down** to reorder the category. You may also change the order of the categories by dragging them around the list using the mouse.

Changing a Story's Category

To change or add a category for a story, edit the story (see "The Editor Screen" on page 87) and click the "Categories" box. A list of all available categories will appear. Select all the categories to which you want to assign the story.

Recording People

Personal Historian lets you assign people to each story to help you organize your personal history. You may assign multiple people to each story, and then filter and select stories based on any group of people.

If you've imported a genealogy (see page 21), the people and relatives that you selected will be included in the file's list of people.

When it comes time to publish the history (see page 141), you have the option of creating an index of people that are referenced in the book. This index is created from the list of people in the file and their stories.

To bring up the list of people in your file, select **Stories > People** from the Main Menu or click the "People" button on the Toolbar.

A list of all persons in the file will appear.

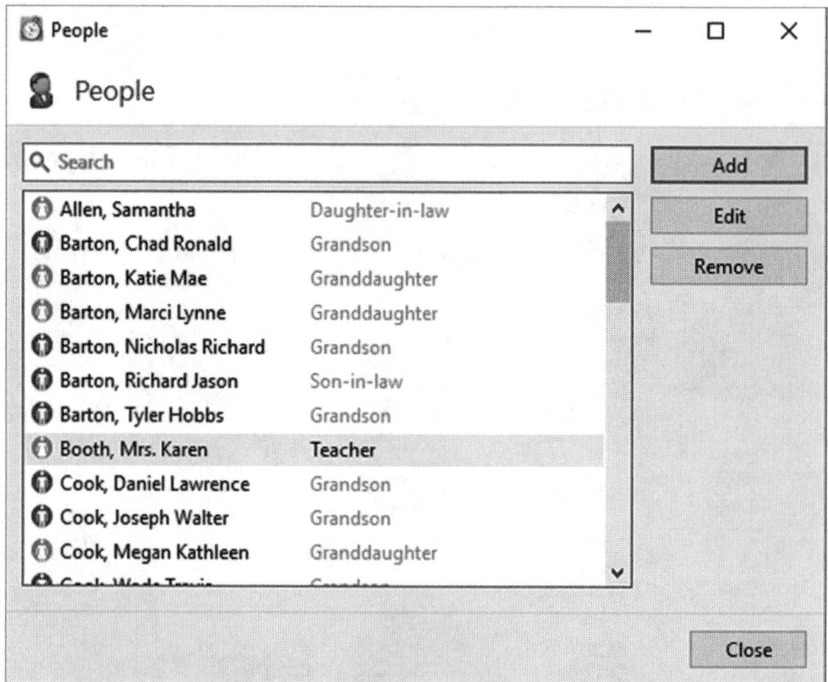

Relationships

One big difference between *Personal Historian* and genealogy software such as *RootsMagic* is the types of people you will record. In your genealogy software, you record all family members including distant relatives.

In *Personal Historian*, you record people that are important to the life of your subject. This will, no doubt, include close family members. But it will also include friends, neighbors, teachers, employers, and other people who played a part in the life stories.

You can record family relationships such as:

- Spouses
- Children
- Great-grandchildren
- Great-great-grandchildren
- Parents
- Grandparents
- Great-grandparents
- Siblings
- Nieces and Nephews
- Aunts and Uncles
- Cousins
- Parents-in-law
- Siblings-in-law
- Children-in-law
- Step-parents
- Half-siblings
- Step-siblings

You can also record non-familial relationships such as:

- Friends
- Neighbors
- Teachers
- Students
- Employers
- Coworkers
- Employees
- Relatives

You can also select "Other" and record any other relationship you like.

Dates of Involvement

Another difference between *Personal Historian* and genealogy software is a person's "Dates of Involvement". This is simply the time in which the person was part of the personal history.

The “Dates of Involvement” are recorded as “Start Date” and “End Date”.

For a family member, it would likely be their dates of birth and death. For a teacher, it could be the time that you were in the teacher’s class. For a friend, it could be the time from you became friends until the day that the friend told the whole school about your unusual birthmark.

Adding a New Person

To add a new person to the file, click the **Add** button to bring up the “Add Person” screen.

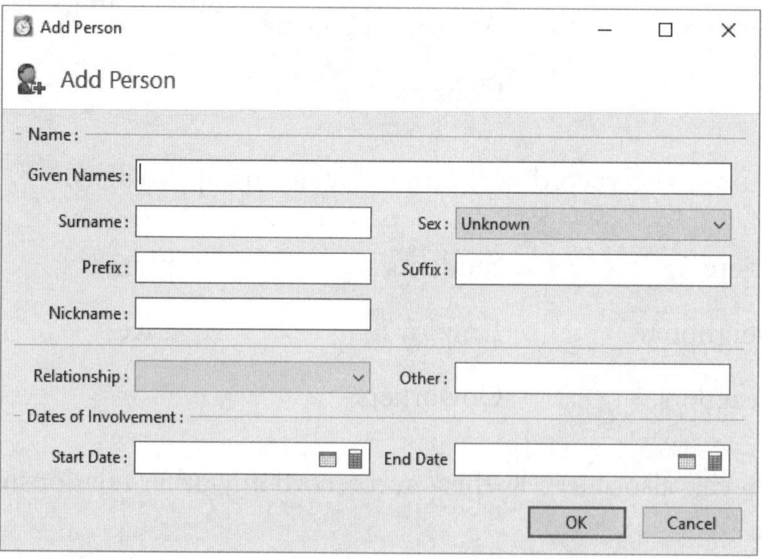

You can enter the name for the new person, as well as their relationship to the history’s subject, and the dates of their involvement in the personal history.

Editing a Person

To edit a person, click the **Edit** button to bring up the "Edit Person" screen.

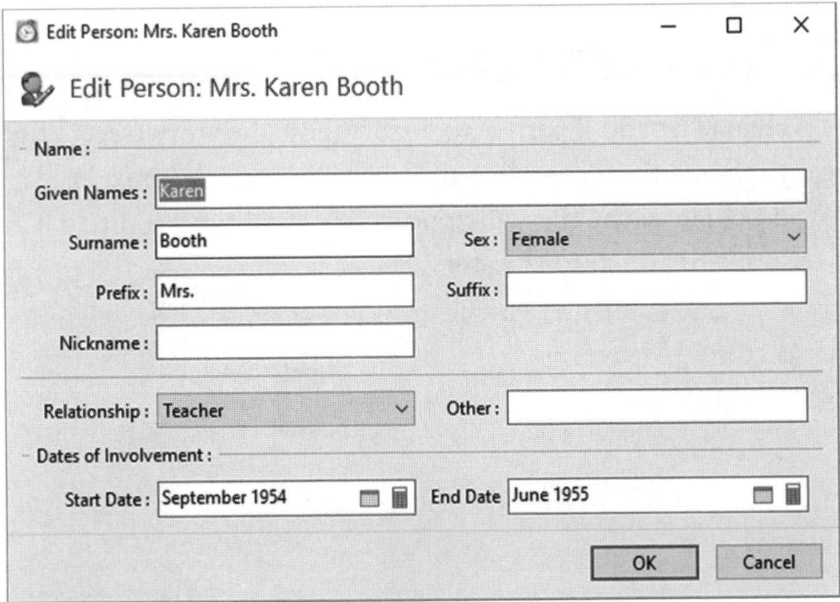

To edit a person, click the **Edit** button on the list of people. Here, you can change any of the original information you entered for the person.

Deleting a Person

To remove a person, click the **Remove** button.

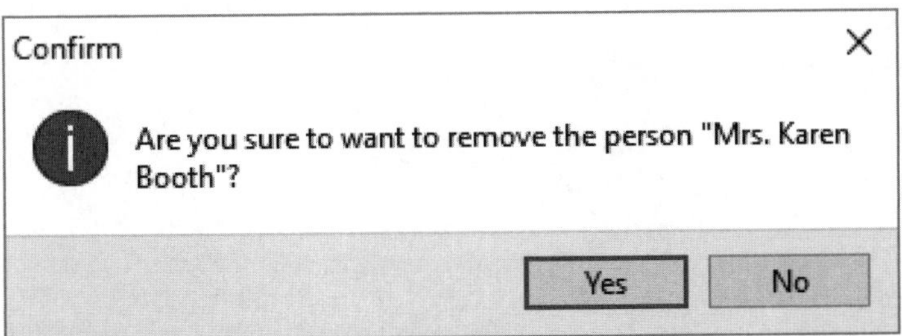

If the person you want to delete is attached to any stories, *Personal Historian* will unattach the person from those stories.

Click **Yes** to confirm the deletion.

Adding a Person to a Story

To change or add a person to a story, edit the story (see "The Editor Screen" on page 87) and click the "People" box. A list of all people in the file will appear. Select all the people that you want to attach to the story.

Tracking Places

Personal Historian lets you assign places to each story to help you organize your personal history. You may assign multiple places to each story, and then filter and select stories based on any group of places (or even all stories within a certain distance of any place). To bring up the list of places in your personal history, select **Stories** > **Places** from the Main Menu.

If you've imported a genealogy (see page 21), the places for events that you selected will be included in the file's list of places.

When it comes time to publish the history (see page 141), you have the option of creating an index of places in the book. This index is created from the list of places in the file and their stories.

To bring up the list of places in your file, select **Stories** > **Places** from the Main Menu or click the "Places" button on the Toolbar.

A list of all places in the file will appear.

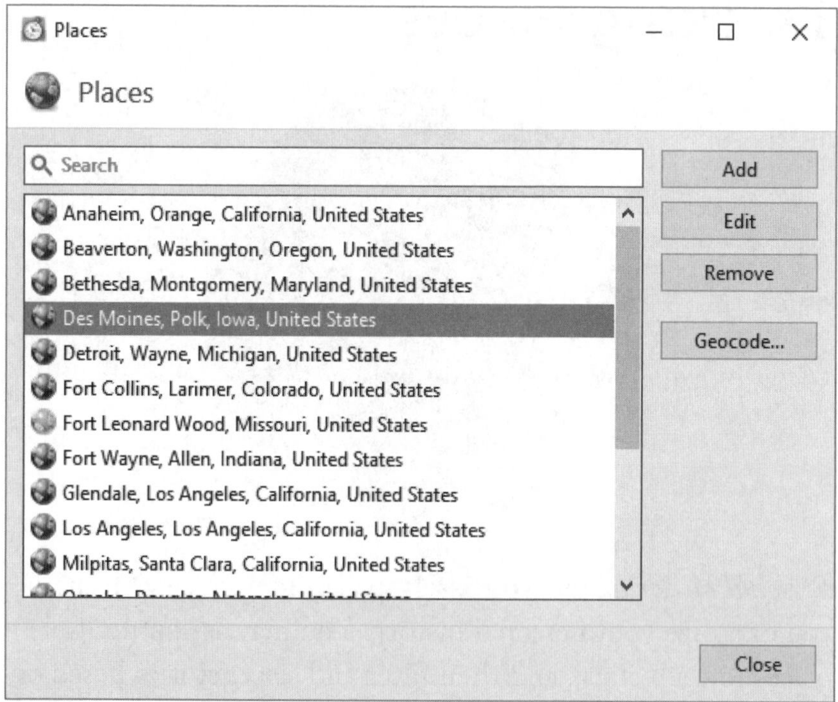

Geocoding Your List of Places

You'll see a small globe next to each place in the list. If the globe is colored, it means that that place has been "geocoded." "Geocoded" is a fancy word for knowing the coordinate (latitude and longitude) for a place. A gray icon means the place has not been geocoded.

You can do some pretty interesting things with a geocoded place, such as filtering stories based on distance from a point. For example, "Show me all stories that took place within 50 miles of Buffalo, New York".

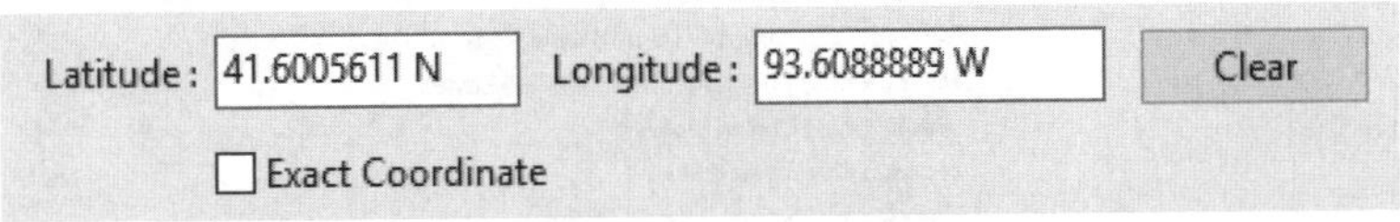

Latitude: 41.6005611 N Longitude: 93.6088889 W Clear

Exact Coordinate

You can add the latitude and longitude when you add or edit a place. Check the **Exact Coordinate** box if the latitude and longitude are for something specific such as a gravesite or hospital. Leave it unchecked if it is for something general such as a city.

If you want to geocode all the places in your file at once, click the **Geocode** button next to the list of places. *Personal Historian* will check its 3.5 million place name database and fill in the latitude and longitude for any places that you haven't already entered that information.

If there are any places that *Personal Historian* can't find and geocode, it will list those places for you to geocode or match manually.

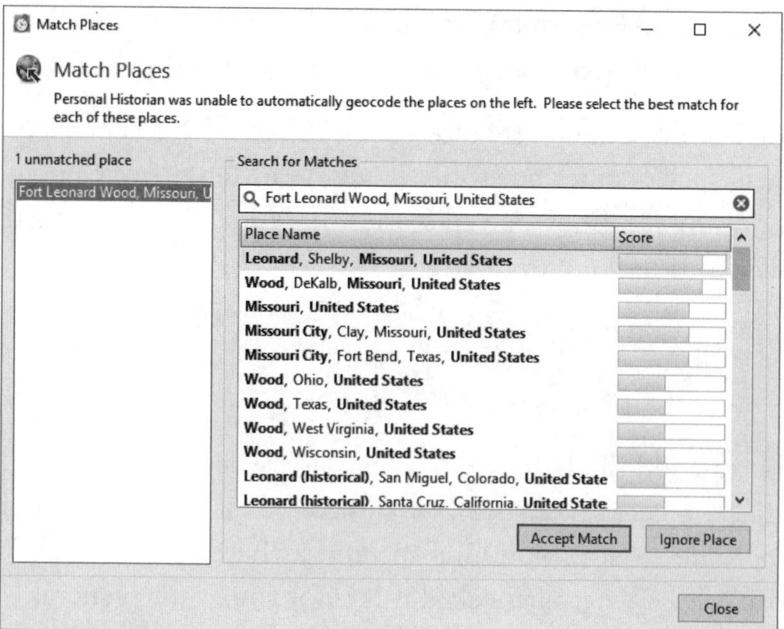

Choose the best match from the list and click **Accept Match**.

Adding a New Place

To add a new place to the file, click the **Add** button to bring up the "Add Place" screen.

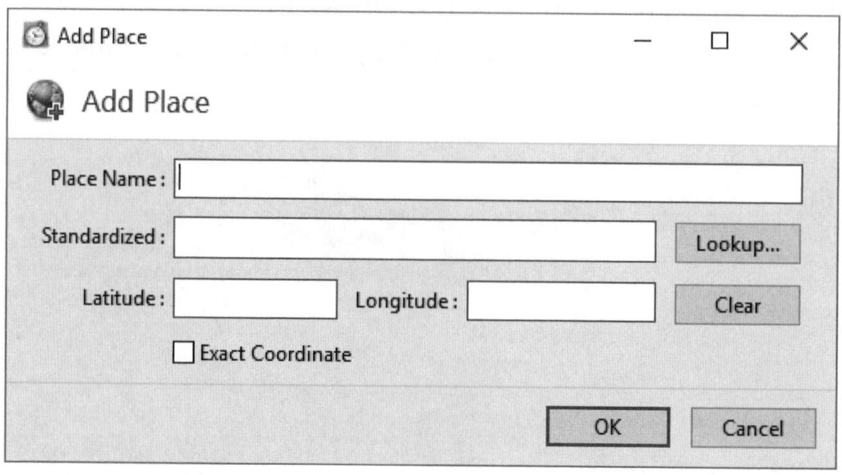

You can enter the name for the new place, as well as the latitude and longitude of the place. If you don't know the coordinates you can click the **Lookup** button and *Personal Historian* will check its 3.5 million place name database for that information.

Editing a Place

To edit a person, click the **Edit** button to bring up the "Edit Place" screen.

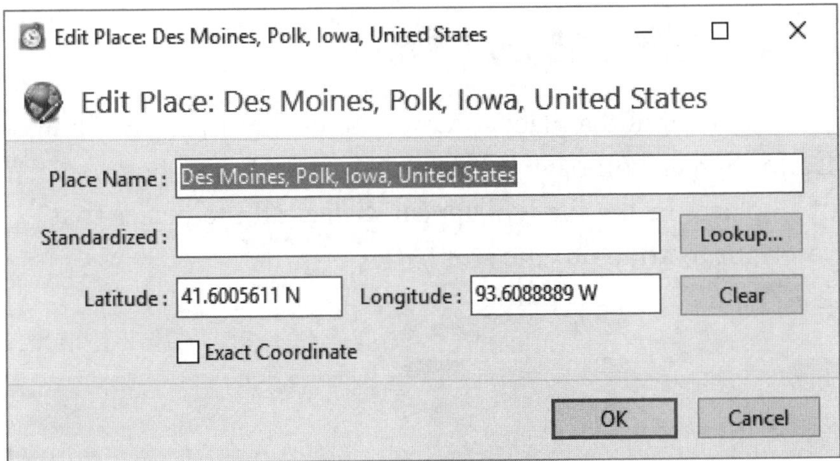

You can edit any of the information you originally entered for the place.

Deleting a Place

To remove a place, click the **Remove** button.

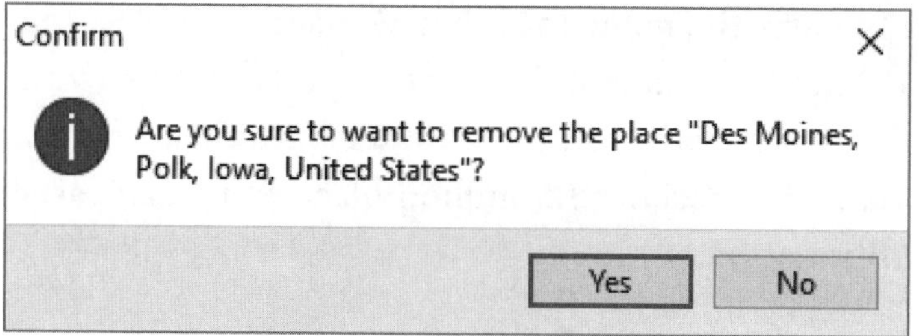

If there are stories that are using the place you want to delete, *Personal Historian* will remove the place from those stories.

Click **Yes** to confirm the deletion.

Changing a Story's Place

To change or add a place to a story, edit the story (see "The Editor Screen" on page 87) and click the "Places" box. A list of all places in the file will appear. Select all the places that you want to attach to the story.

The Editor Screen

The Editor Screen is where the thinking, brainstorming, organizing, and actual writing is done. Every story will open up in the editor. You can open the editor by adding or editing a story (see page 63).

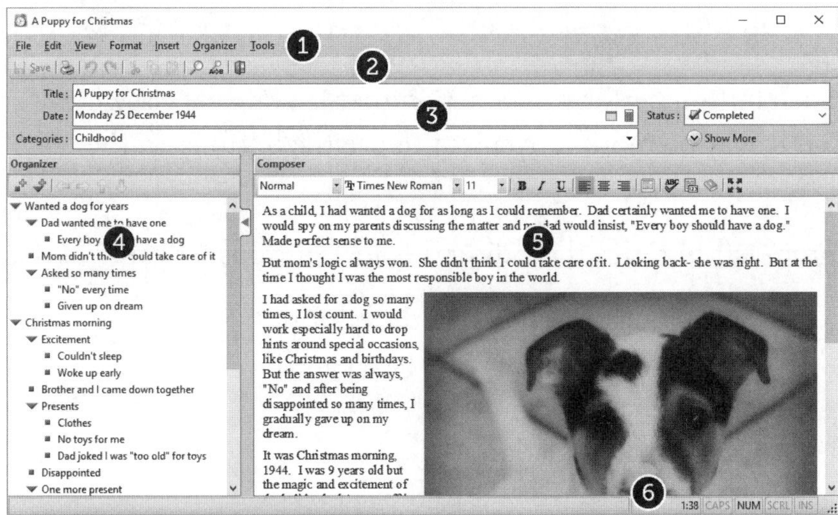

The Edit Screen consists of:

1. Editor Menu
2. Editor Toolbar
3. Story Information
4. Organizer
5. Composer
6. Editor Status Bar

Editor Menu

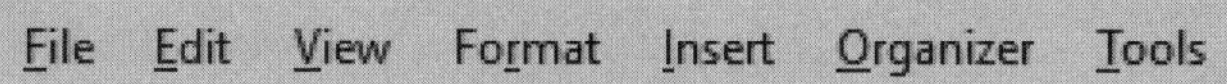

The Editor Menu provides access to the many features of the editor. Click on any menu item to choose from a dropdown menu. Most options from the Editor Menu are also available by clicking a button on the Editor Toolbar or by using a shortcut key (see page 183).

Editor Toolbar

The Editor Toolbar is a set of icons just below the menu in the Editor Screen.

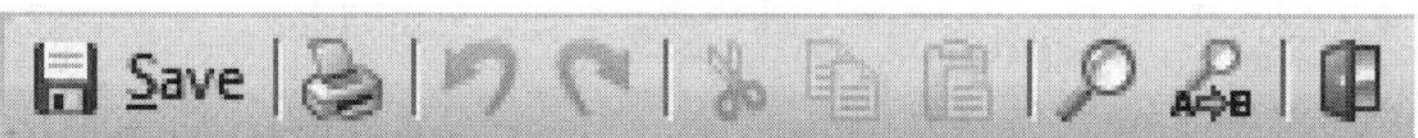

Each button performs a function that is available elsewhere, but it may be more convenient to use the buttons on the Editor Toolbar.

From left to right, the Editor Toolbar buttons let you:

- Save the story and close the editor
- Print or export the story (see page 157)
- Undo the last action
- Redo the last action
- Cut the selected text to the clipboard
- Copy the selected text to the clipboard
- Paste text from the clipboard
- Search for text
- Search and replace text
- Close the editor

Editor Status Bar

The Editor Status Bar is located at the bottom of the Editor Screen.

The four boxes on the right of the Editor Status Bar show whether the Caps Lock, Number Lock, Scroll Lock, and Insert Mode are on (black) or off (greyed-out).

The fifth box is a timer, showing you how much time has elapsed since you opened the Editor Screen.

Story Information

The Story Information panel rests at the top of the screen, below the Editor Toolbar.

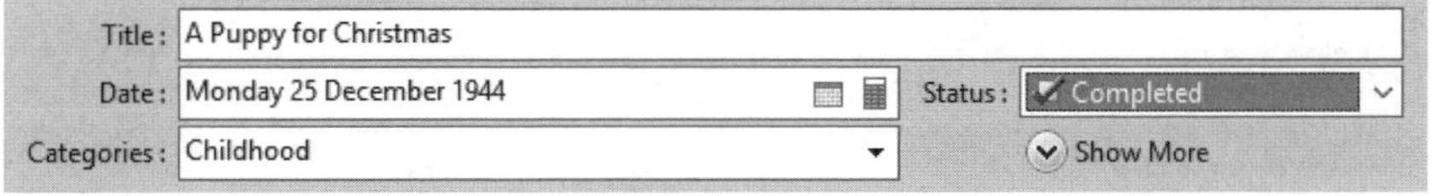

The Story Information is where you enter details about the story, such as the title, dates, categories, people and places, status and your rating for the story.

To free up more space for the Organizer and Composer, the Story Information panel hides the less-critical half of its information. This includes the story's age, sort date, rating, people, and places.

Click on the **Show More** button to show this information.

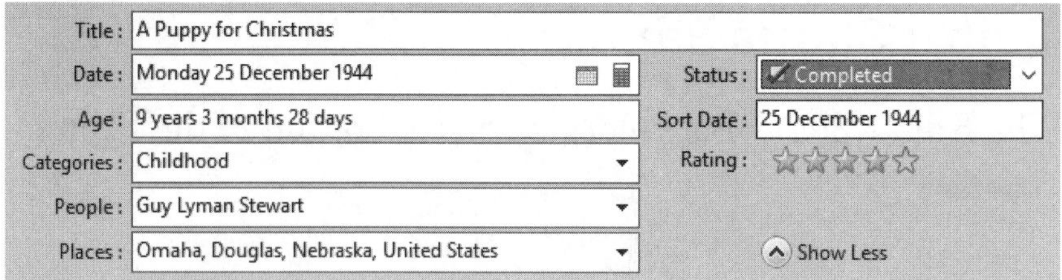

Title : A Puppy for Christmas
Date : Monday 25 December 1944
Status : Completed
Age : 9 years 3 months 28 days
Sort Date : 25 December 1944
Categories : Childhood
Rating :
People : Guy Lyman Stewart
Places : Omaha, Douglas, Nebraska, United States
Show Less

Click on the **Show Less** button to hide it again, freeing up screen space.

Change the name of the story in the title box. Use the stars to give the story a rating between 0 and 5. The story's status (see page 64) can also be set here.

When you enter either the date or age, *Personal Historian* will calculate the other one.

There is also a "sort date" that doesn't print but tells *Personal Historian* how to sort the stories on the Main Screen when you sort the stories chronologically. *Personal Historian* will automatically fill out the sort date for you when you enter something in the date box. You can manually change the sort date later if you like.

Use the corresponding boxes to assign categories (page 69), people (page 75), and places (page 81) to the story.

The Organizer

The Organizer is one of *Personal Historian*'s most powerful tools, yet it is also one of its most underutilized tools. It is located in the lower-left portion of the Editor Screen.

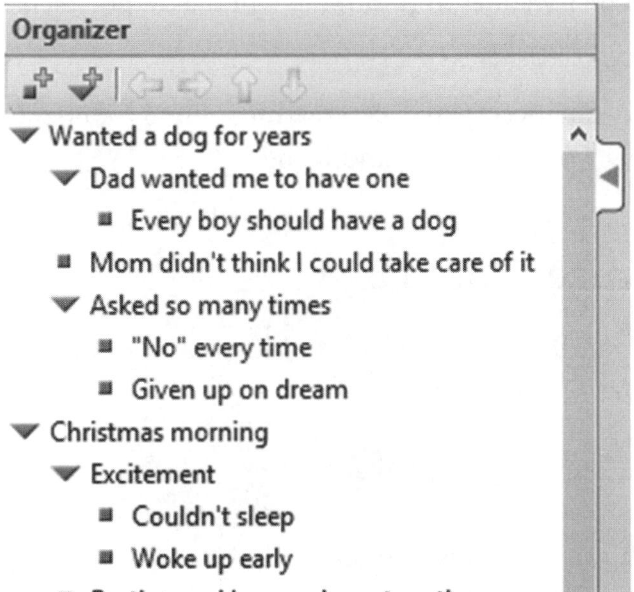

The Organizer is the place where you collect the facts, feelings, ideas, and memories before you begin writing. It can be used as an outliner, a brainstorming tool (see page 99), or even just a scratch pad.

Most people tend to skip over the Organizer and jump right into the writing. Sadly, they miss out on some pretty amazing benefits.

Effectively using the Organizer will help you:

1. **Save Time** – Yes, it's true. By brainstorming, organizing, and outlining your ideas in advance, the actual writing process will go much faster and more smoothly.
2. **Remember Details** – Brainstorming is a proven method for helping you recall memories and details that may otherwise be lost.
3. **Write Clearly and Understandably** – Your writing won't wander and ramble, will make more sense, and will flow better.

Are you convinced yet? Keep reading. The Organizer is definitely worth learning and using.

Organizer Toolbar

The Organizer Toolbar is a set of icons at the top of the Organizer on the Editor Screen.

Each button performs a function that is available elsewhere, but it may be more convenient to use the buttons on the Organizer Toolbar.

From left to right, the Organizer Toolbar buttons let you:

- Add a new Organizer item (see page 94)

- Add a new Organizer subitem (see page 94)
- Move an item to the left (see page 95)
- Move an item to the right (see page 95)
- Move an item up (see page 95)
- Move an item down (see page 95)

Organizer Items

As in an outline, the Organizer works with lists of items that can be grouped together.

- Christmas morning
  - Excitement
    - Couldn't sleep
    - Woke up early
  - Brother and I came down together

For example, in the figure above, the item "Christmas morning" has two subitems- "Excitement" and "Brother and I came down together" which are grouped together beneath it.

"Excitement" itself has two subitems beneath it while "Brother and I" has no subitems.

Next to each Organizer item is one of three possible icons:

■ The item has no subitems

▶ The item has subitems but they are currently hidden

▼ The item has subitems and they are currently visible

▶ Adding a New Item

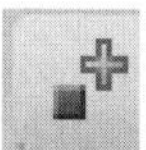

To add a new item directly under the currently selected item in the Organizer:

1. While in the Organizer, press **Enter**.
2. Type in the text for the new item.

▶ Adding a New Subitem

To add a new subitem to the currently selected item in the Organizer:

1. While in the Organizer, press **Alt** + **Enter**.
2. Type in the text for the new subitem.

▶ Editing an Item

To edit the text of an Organizer item:

1. Select the item in the Organizer that you wish to edit.
2. Simply start typing if you wish to replace the text or press **F2** if you wish to modify the text.

▶ Deleting Items

To delete items from the Organizer:

1. Select the item or items (see "Selecting Multiple Items at Once" on page 96) that you wish to delete.
2. Press the **Delete** key.
3. If asked to confirm the deletion, click **Yes**.

▶ Expanding and Collapsing an Item

If an Organizer item has subitems that are hidden (shown by the ▸ icon), you can make its subitems visible, or "expand" the item by clicking on the icon or by pressing **+** on the numeric keypad of your keyboard.

If an Organizer item has subitems that are visible (shown by the ▼ icon), you can hide its subitems, or "collapse" the item by clicking on the icon or by pressing - on the numeric keypad of your keyboard.

Moving Organizer Items

After creating several Organizer items, you may want to reorder them or arrange them into groups.

To move Organizer items, first select the item or items (see "Selecting Multiple Items at Once" on page 96) that you wish to move.

> When an item is moved up and down in the Organizer, all of its subitems will also move with it.

There are three ways of moving the selected item(s):

1. **Keyboard** - Hold down the **Alt** key while you press an **Arrow Key** corresponding with the direction that you want to move the item(s).

   The **Up** and **Down** arrows are used to move the items higher of lower in the list of items.

   The **Right** arrow is used to make the item a child of the item above it. (Sometimes called demotion.)

   The **Left** arrow is used to change a child to the same level as its parent. (Sometimes called promotion.)

2. **Mouse** - Move the mouse pointer over the item(s), hold down the mouse button, drag the item(s) to their new location, and release the mouse button.

3. **Toolbar** – Click the Organizer Toolbar buttons with the direction that you want to move the item(s).

Selecting Multiple Items at Once

There are times when you will want to select more than one item in the Organizer (such as deleting or moving items).

To select more than one item:

1. Click on the first item that you want to select.
2. Hold down the **Ctrl** key and click on all of the other items that you want to select.
3. Each item that you click on will be selected.

To select a continuous block of items:

1. Click on the top-most item that you want to select.
2. Hold down the **Shift** key and click on the bottom-most item that you want to select.
3. All items from the top-most item to the bottom-most item will be selected.

You can also combine the **Ctrl** and **Shift** keys to select multiple continuous blocks of items.

Copy Items to the Composer

Once you have used the Organizer to plan your writing, you may wish to use a copy of your work to begin writing in the Composer.

To copy the contents of the Organizer into the Composer, select **Organizer** > **Copy to Composer** from the Editor Menu. When asked if you really want to copy the items, click **Yes**.

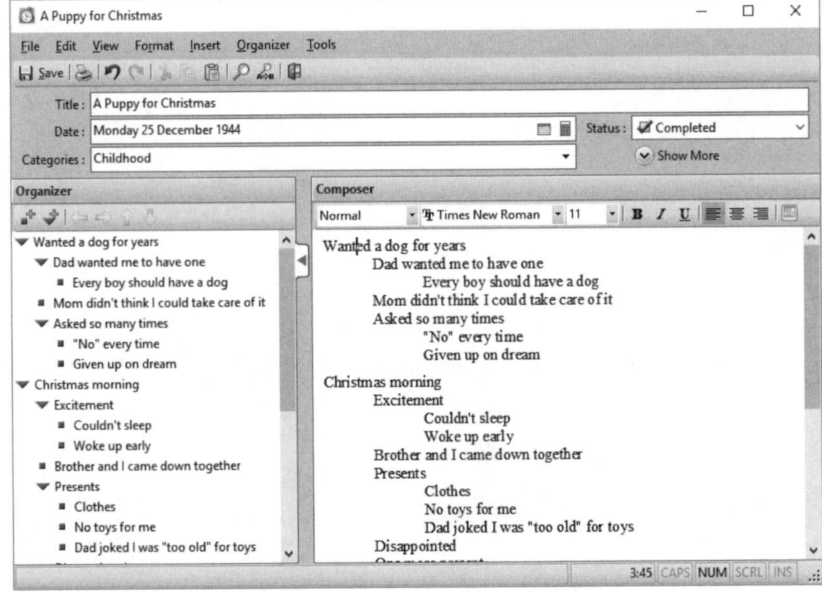

The Memory Solution

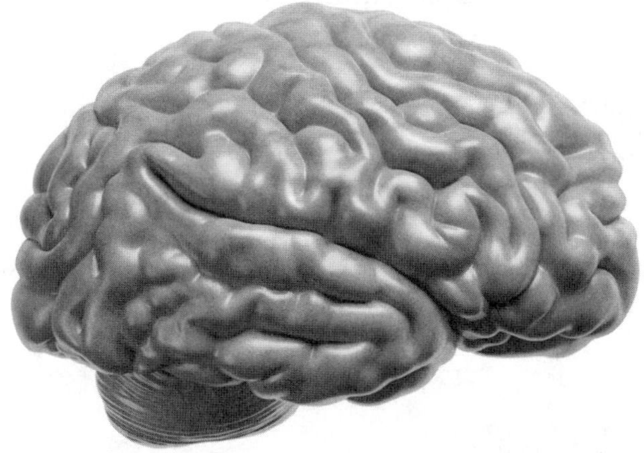

Is your memory (or lack thereof) holding you back from writing your life stories? If so, this section is just for you. I'm going to show you how to use the Organizer tool (see page 91) to remember those impossible details.

Interested? Read on.

Brainstorming

The secret is "brainstorming". You may already be familiar with brainstorming as a way of thinking up ideas, plans, solutions, and more. Turns out, it's remarkably good at helping you recall memories and details that would otherwise be forgotten.

I've taught brainstorming using *Personal Historian's* Organizer tool to thousands of people. I'll often hear from users who've experimented with it and are astonished at the results. As one person put it, "I remembered things I'd forgotten that I had forgotten!"

If brainstorming seems difficult at first, don't give up. It may take a little time and practice, but the rewards are worth it.

The four steps of brainstorming are:

1. Visualize
2. Summarize
3. Organize
4. Repeat

Let's demonstrate these four steps with a little example. Imagine that we are writing about "My First Date."

Step 1: Visualize

The first step is to "visualize" and think of everything you can about the story, topic or event. Think of the "who", "what", "when", "where", "why", and "how".

Ponder on the five senses. What do you see, hear, smell, touch, and taste? Concentrate on the emotions. What were your feelings? What were the feelings of others?

As we visualize "My First Date", we think about our date, her family, and the cool fall Saturday night. We remember the restaurant where we ate, the school gymnasium that hosted the dance, why we chose this particular date, how we asked her to go, and how we were transported throughout the evening.

We think of the bright lights at the dance, the music of the live band, the smell of our date's perfume, wiping our sweaty palms on our suit coat, and the taste of the watered-down punch.

We remember how nervous we were as we picked her up from her home, how awkward we both felt at dinner, how happy she was to see her friends at the dance, and how relieved we felt when it was all over.

Step 2: Summarize

The next step is to capture all the details that we've visualized and enter them into the Organizer (see page 91). Some rules for this step:

- Keep each item brief, no more than 3-4 words. Do not write complete sentences.
- Don't worry about spelling. This isn't our actual writing.
- Don't worry about if you'll actually use it. You can erase items later.
- Don't worry about order, grouping, or if it even makes any sense.

You're essentially trying to hook a fire hose between your brain and *Personal Historian*. You want to keep the water flowing as quickly and smoothly as possible. Worrying about sentences, spelling, and usefulness is just putting kinks in the hose.

Our Organizer will now look something like this:

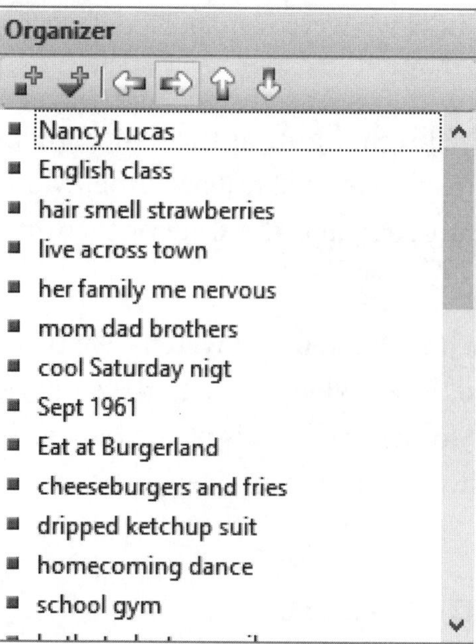

There is an interesting thing about our memories. We often can't remember any details of an event and yet, when we start brainstorming, one ever-so-tiny thought can trigger a flood of new memories. Jot down each of them.

Just keep writing down those thoughts until you absolutely can't come up with another one. Then move on to step 3.

Step 3: Organize

The next step is to "Organize" the items or to arrange them into logical groups and a logical order.

▶ Grouping

Grouping finds areas that are common to items in the Organizer. The common items are brought together as subitems in a common group.

To group items:

1. Look at the items in your list and consider which ones belong together.

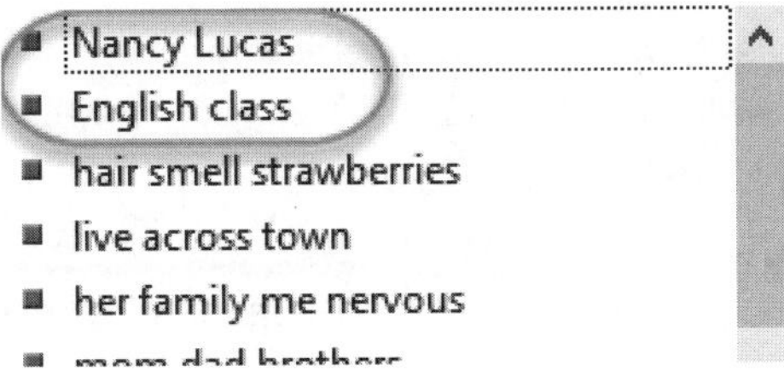

2. Create a new item and give it a name that describes what the previous items have in common. This will be your group heading.

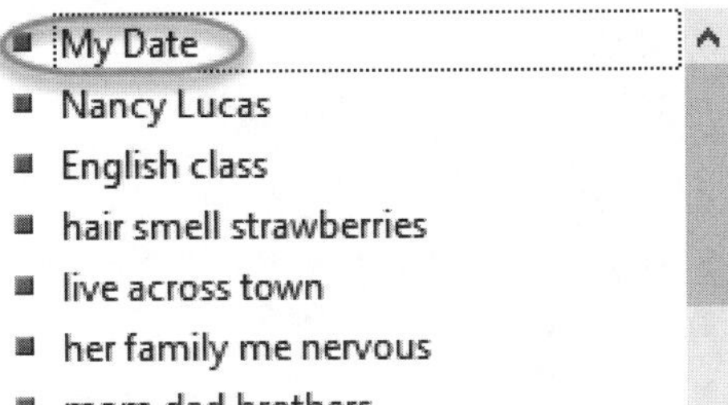

3. Move the two items, as children, under the new group heading (see “Moving Organizer Items” on page 95).

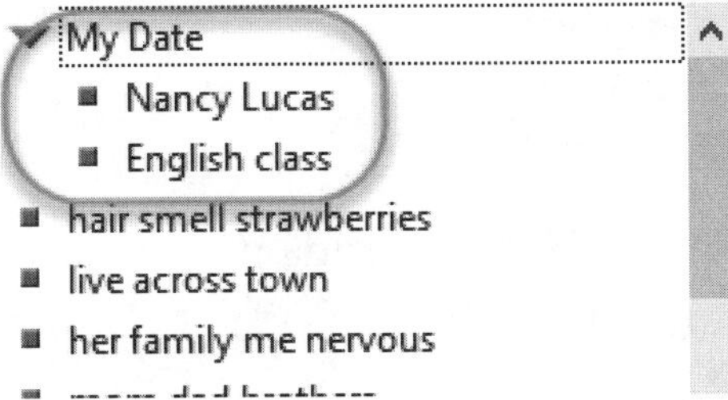

4. Search through the remaining items to see if any others could belong to the new group. If you find any, move them as the group heading.

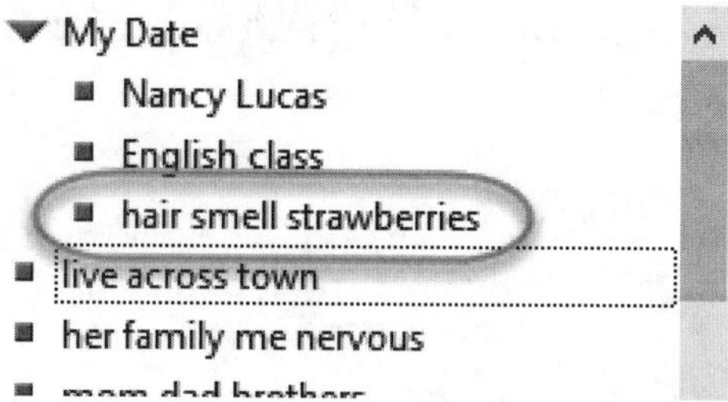

5. Collapse the group heading so that the subitems are not visible. This simplifies the list of items.

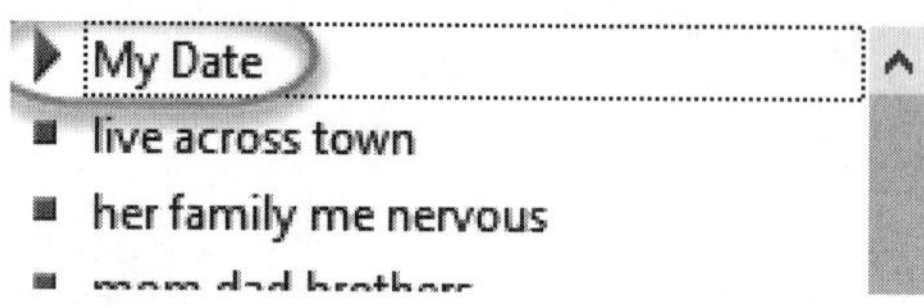

6. Continue grouping items in the list.

My Date
Her family
The Night
Dinner
homecoming dance
Why her
ask her go
transportation
pick her up
goodnight

If an item doesn't fit and we decide not to use it, we can simply delete it (see page 94).

▶ Ordering

Ordering determines which items (or groups) appear before others. We want the items to be in an order that will help the reader to understand the finished story.

1. Rearrange all of the first level of items and groups first.

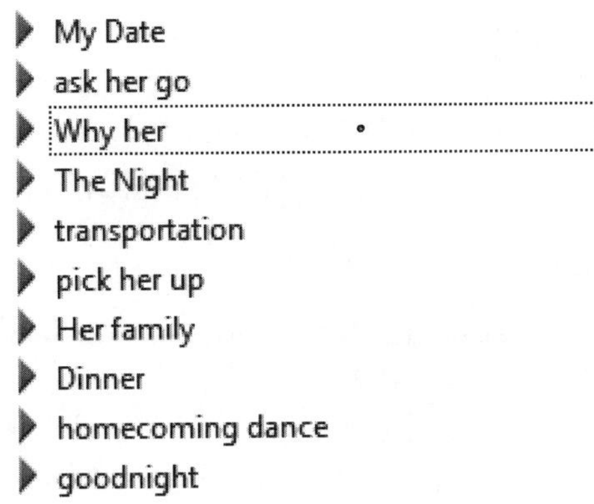

2. Expand each group and reorder the subitems and groups within it.

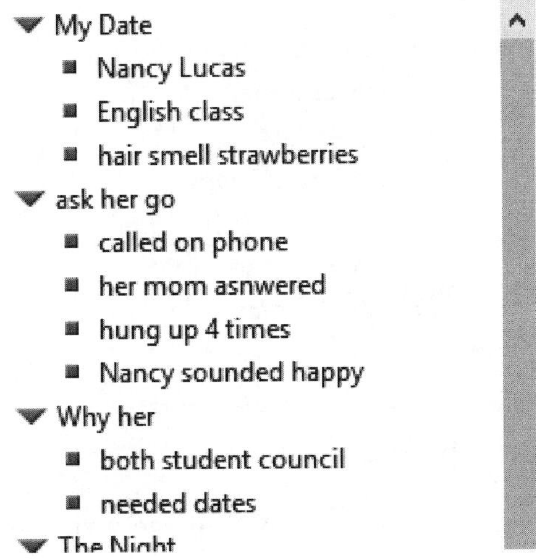

My Date
Nancy Lucas
English class
hair smell strawberries
ask her go
called on phone
her mom asnwered
hung up 4 times
Nancy sounded happy
Why her
both student council
needed dates

Step 4: Repeat

Now we go back to Step 1 and repeat the whole process. We add more items as more details come to mind. We group them together and arrange them in a logical order.

At some point, the fire hose runs dry. When you're satisfied with your work, the brainstorming process is complete.

The "O" Word

So now you've gone through the process of brainstorming. Look closely at the Organizer now. What do you see?

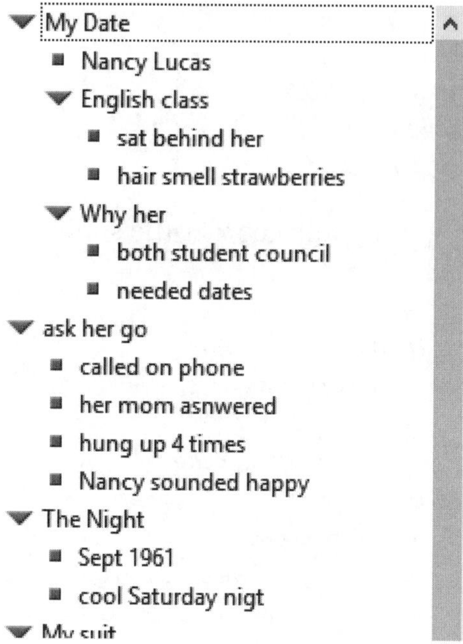

That's right- an "outline". The dreaded "O" Word from Junior High English class.

My English teacher would insist that we write an outline before we wrote our essays. I <u>hated</u> it. It seemed like a waste of time to have to write my essay twice! I just wanted to dive right in and just write my paper.

Well, guess what- my English teacher was right. Making an outline before you write actually saves time. We can now write our story in the Composer on the right while looking out our outline on the left.

Don't pause trying to figure out what to write next. No copying and pasting as we rearrange sentences and paragraphs. Just fleshing out the skeleton we already made. Best of all, you've hopefully conquered the memory problem.

Hopefully through brainstorming, you too will remember things that you've forgotten that you've forgotten.

The Composer

The Composer is where the real work begins. It's where you write the actual story.

It is a word processor that includes text formatting and alignment, photographs, documents, horizontal lines, spell check, thesaurus, and Readability Check.

It takes up the lower-right portion of the Editor Screen.

Composer Toolbar

The Composer Toolbar is a set of boxes and icons at the top of the Composer on the Editor Screen.

The first three boxes allow you to adjust the style (page 61), font, and size of the text in the Composer.

Each button performs a function that is available elsewhere, but it may be more convenient to use the buttons on the Composer Toolbar.

From left to right, the Composer Toolbar buttons let you:

- Bold/unbold the text
- Italicize/un-italicize the text
- Underline/un-underline the text
- Left-justify the text
- Center the text
- Right-justify the text
- Insert a picture (see page 112)
- Spell Check (see page 116)
- Readability Check (see page 119)
- Thesaurus (see page 118)
- Toggle fullscreen mode (see page 123)

Applying Styles

Personal Historian lets you create "styles" (see "Styles" on page 61). A style is a combination of font typeface and size, text formatting, and paragraph settings (such as indent and spacing).

To use a style, just place your cursor in a paragraph and select the desired style from the style drop list.

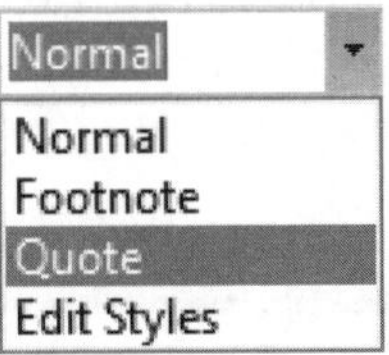

You can add or edit styles by selecting **Edit Styles** from the list.

Fonts & Formatting

To change the font for some text, highlight the text (by clicking and dragging the highlight) and select the font from the drop list of font typefaces.

You can also change the size of the font from the drop list of font sizes.

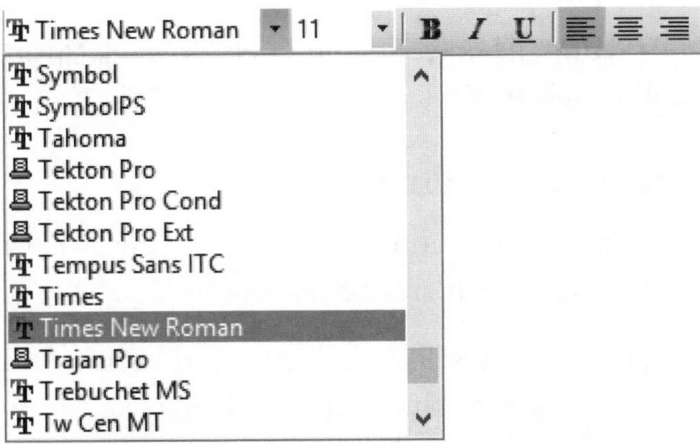

> Although, *Personal Historian* allows you to use multiple fonts within your story, it is better to use styles (see page 61) so that you can easily change the look of certain types of text for all stories at once.

The Composer also allows you to format and stylize your text. You can bold, italicize, and underline the text. You can also adjust the alignment of a paragraph to left-aligned, centered, or right-aligned.

Adding Pictures

To add a photo or graphic to a story, select **Insert** > **Picture** from the Editor Menu or click the **Insert Picture** Toolbar button. A file selection screen will appear.

Choose the type of file you wish to import from the "Files of Type" list. *Personal Historian* can read these most common graphics formats:

- Bitmap Image File (.bmp)
- JPEG Image Files (.jpg, .jpeg)
- GIF Images (.gif)
- PNG Images (.png)

Select the picture file on your computer and click **Open**. The picture will be inserted into the Composer.

▶ Resizing and Moving Pictures

Once a picture has been added to the Composer, you can easily resize it or move it around the story.

Click on the picture to select it. You'll see that tiny square "handles" will appear on the corners and edges of the picture. Drag the handles with the mouse to resize the picture.

You'll also see that the Composer Toolbar changes to "Picture Tools".

The Picture Tools allow you to change the alignment/wrapping of the picture. You can choose between:

Treat the Picture as a Character

But mom's logic always won. She didn't think I could take care of it. Looking back- she was right. But at the time I thought I was the most responsible boy in the world.

I had asked for a dog so many times, I lost count. I would work especially hard to drop hints around special occasions, like Christmas and birthdays. But the answer was always, "No" and after being disappointed so many times, I gradually gave up on my dream.

It was Christmas morning, 1944. I was 9 years old but the magic and excitement of the holiday hadn't worn off in the least. Sarah and I had a hard time falling asleep the night before but that didn't stop us from waking up at 5 a.m. We impatiently waited

Align Picture to the Left

But mom's logic always won. She didn't think I could take care of it. Looking back- she was right. But at the time I thought I was the most responsible boy in the world.

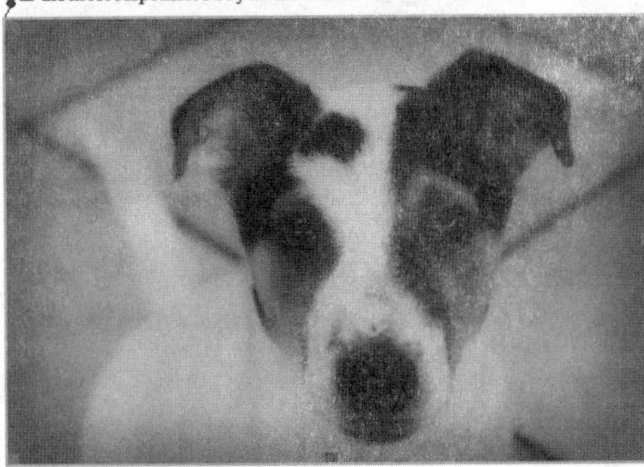

I had asked for a dog so many times, I lost count. I would work especially hard to drop hints around special occasions, like Christmas and birthdays. But the answer was always, "No" and after being disappointed so many times, I gradually gave up on my dream.

It was Christmas morning, 1944. I was 9 years old but the magic and excitement of the holiday hadn't worn off in the least. Sarah and I had a hard time falling asleep the night before but that didn't stop us from waking up at 5 a.m. We impatiently waited while mom and dad woke up and mom fed the baby.

Finally, it was time to go downstairs to see what Santa had brought us and to open our presents. I don't remember much about my presents that year. I know I got some clothes and probably some books. But I do remember that I did not get any toys. Dad joked, "You're getting a little old for toys." I tried to hide my disappointment as I secretly wanted toys but wanted to appear to be as mature as dad had thought I was.

All the presents had been opened and we started to clean up the wrapping paper. I was trying but doing a poor job of hiding my

Center the Picture (Default)

Picture Tools

But mom's logic always won. She didn't think I could take care of it. Looking back- she was right. But at the time I thought I was the most responsible boy in the world.

I had asked for a dog so many times, I lost count. I would work especially hard to drop hints around special occasions, like Christmas and birthdays. But the answer was always, "No" and after being disappointed so many times, I gradually gave up on my

Align Picture to the Right

Picture Tools

But mom's logic always won. She didn't think I could take care of it. Looking back- she was right. But at the time I thought I was the most responsible boy in the world.

I had asked for a dog so many times, I lost count. I would work especially hard to drop hints around special occasions, like Christmas and birthdays. But the answer was always, "No" and after being disappointed so many times, I gradually gave up on my dream.

It was Christmas morning, 1944. I was 9 years old but the magic and excitement of the holiday hadn't worn off in the least. Sarah and I had a hard time falling asleep the night before but that didn't stop us from waking up at 5 a.m. We impatiently waited while mom and dad woke up and mom fed the baby.

Finally, it was time to go downstairs to see what Santa had brought us and to open our presents. I don't remember much about my presents that year. I know I got some clothes and probably some books. But I do remember that I did not get any toys. Dad joked, "You're getting a little old for toys." I tried to hide my disappointment as I secretly wanted toys but wanted to appear to be as mature as dad had thought I was.

All the presents had been opened and we started to clean up the wrapping paper. I was trying but doing a poor job of hiding my

Once you've sized and positioned the picture, click anywhere in the text to remove the handles and return to the regular Organizer Toolbar.

▶ Adding Picture from the Clipboard

It is also possible to paste pictures from a word processor or web browser into the Composer via the clipboard. To do so:

1. In a web browser or word processor, copy the picture to the clipboard.
2. In *Personal Historian*, open the Editor Screen and place the cursor in the Composer.
3. Select **Edit** > **Paste** from the Editor Menu, click the **Paste** button on the Editor Toolbar, or press **Ctrl** + **V** on the keyboard.

Importing a Document

If you've written a story in a word processor such as Microsoft Word, you may want to import that into a story. *Personal Historian* can import a Rich Text File (.rtf) which can be saved from your word processor or publishing program.

To import a document into the Composer:

1. From the Editor Menu, select **File** > **Import**. A file selection screen will appear.
2. Choose the type of file you wish to import from the "Files of Type" list. Choose "Rich Text Files (*.rtf)"
3. Find the document on your computer.
4. Click **Open**.

The file will be inserted into the Composer.

> Rather than saving a Rich Text File from your word processor and importing it into *Personal Historian*, you may find it faster to simply copy the story and pictures from your word processor to the clipboard and paste it into *Personal Historian's* Composer.

Spell Check & Thesaurus

Personal Historian includes several tools, standard to any writing software, that will improve your writing.

▶ Live Spell Check

The Live Spell Check will let you know if you've misspelled a word as soon as you've typed it. Just look for the little red squiggle.

I realy enjoy using Personal Historian!

If you see a misspelled word, right-click on it with the mouse to see a menu of suggested spellings.

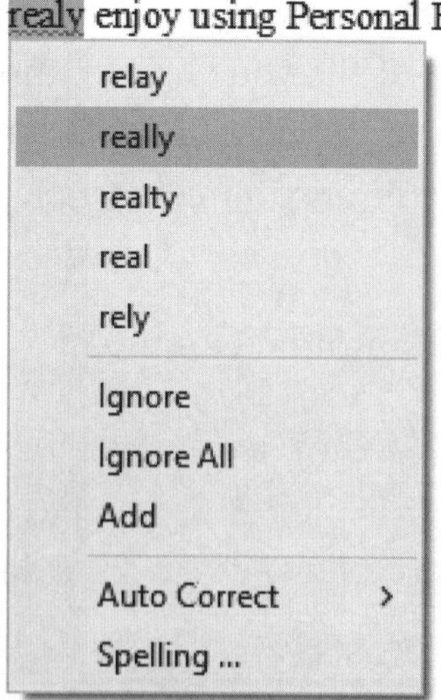

Click on the correct spelling from the menu. If the word is not misspelled (common with names), click **Ignore All** from the menu.

The Live Spell Check can be turned on and off by selecting **Tools** > **Live Spell Check** from the Editor Menu.

▶ Manual Spell Check

The Manual Spell Check lets you perform a spell check at your convenience. To run it, select **Tools** > **Spell Check** from the Editor Menu, click the **Spell Check** button on the Composer Toolbar, or press **F7** on the keyboard.

If any misspelled words are found you'll see the spell check screen:

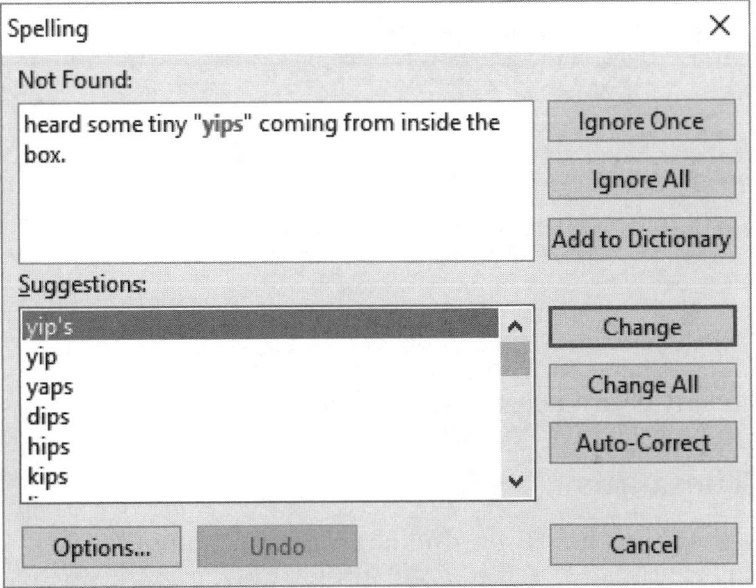

Select the correct spelling from the list of suggestions and click **Change**. If the word is not misspelled (common with names), click **Ignore Once**, **Ignore All**, or **Add to Dictionary** from the menu.

▶ Configure Spell Check

You can adjust spell check settings and even languages by select **Tools** > **Configure Spell Check** from the Editor Menu.

The Spelling Options screen will appear:

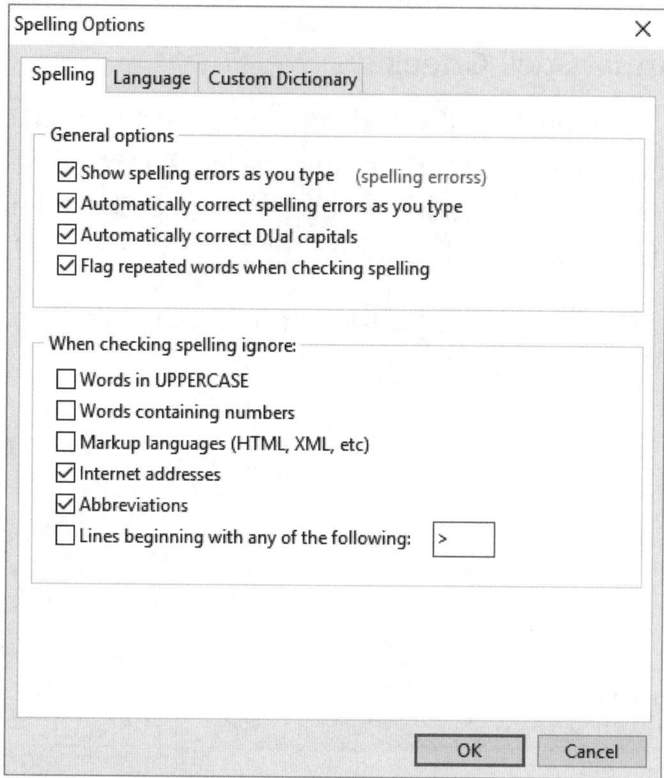

Make any desired changes and click **OK**.

▶ Thesaurus

The thesaurus helps you find alternate (and often better) words than you originally used. This can be a powerful way to find the right word for a situation.

To use the thesaurus, just select the word you want to examine. You can do this by either double-clicking on the word or by dragging the mouse over the word to highlight it. Once the word is highlighted, click on the **Thesaurus** button on the Composer Toolbar, choose **Tools** > **Thesaurus** from the Editor Menu, or press **Shift** + **F7** on the keyboard.

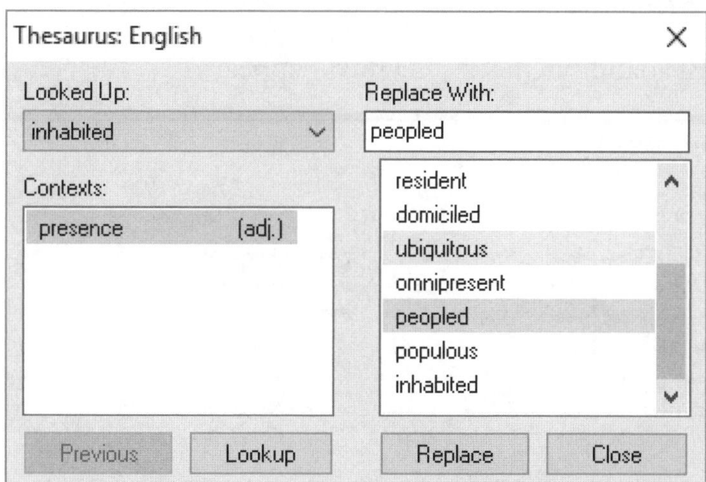

The Thesaurus screen presents words that are similar to or related to the word that you selected. Not all the words presented have the same meaning as the word you selected. Some will have a slightly different meaning, and some will be loosely related to the original word.

Choose a replacement word and then click **Replace**.

See "Finding the Right Word" on page 131 for tips on how to better use the thesaurus in your writing.

Readability Check

The purpose of the Readability Check is to get a general feel for how readable your writing will be to others. It does this by looking at the size of your words, the length of your sentences, and the number of unique words used. It does not attempt to check grammar or make a statement about the quality of your writing and its content.

To perform a Readability Check, select **Tools** > **Readability Check** from the Editor Menu, click the **Readability Check** button on the Composer toolbar, or press **Alt** + **F7** on the keyboard.

The Readability Check screen will appear:

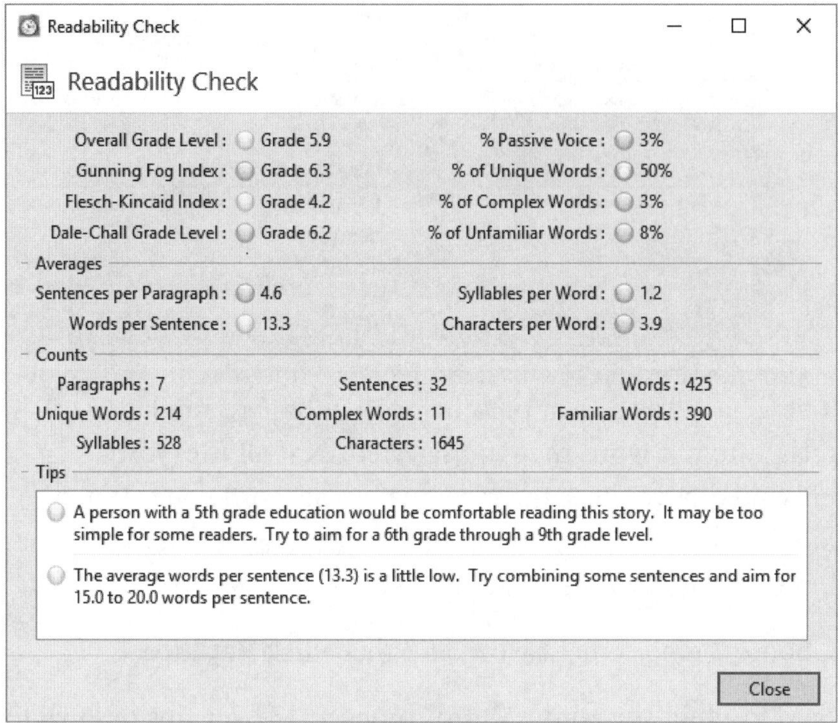

▶ Statistics

The screen will show you a plethora of counts, averages, and percentages. These will likely only appeal to people like me, who majored in statistics at college.

▶ Grade Level

Using the statistics mentioned above, *Personal Historian* uses several different formulas that estimate the writing's "grade level". The grade level <u>does not</u> reflect your intelligence or level of schooling. It <u>does</u> try to estimate what level of education a person would need to be comfortable reading the story.

The "Overall Grade Level" is a composite of three other calculations: the Gunning Fog Index, Flesch-Kinkaid Index, and Dale-Chall Grade Level.

▶ Tips

If numbers aren't your thing, forget everything else and just look at the "Tips" section on the bottom of the Readability Check screen.

Based on the calculations, the tips are plain-English suggestions on how to improve the readability of your writing and make it easier for your audience to understand and enjoy.

For an example of how to effectively use the Readability Check to make your writing better, see "Make it Readable" on page 126.

Dictating and Reading Back Your Story

Personal Historian can use your Windows computer's built-in speech recognition and text-to-speech engines. They allow you to dictate text to *Personal Historian* via a microphone and to have a story read back to you aloud.

> Because these features rely entirely upon the Windows operating system, their performance on Windows emulation software (such as on a Mac computer) may vary.

▶ Read to Me

It can sometimes be useful to hear a story read back to you by someone else; especially to determine if it sounds or flows naturally.

To have *Personal Historian* read a story or text selection back to you, select **Tools** > **Read to Me** from the Editor Menu.

Press any key or click the mouse to stop the reading.

▶ Dictate Text

There are occasions where dictating your story with a microphone can be a huge time saver: transcribing journals or letters, reciting a story from memory, or difficulty typing with a keyboard.

To begin speech recognition, make sure your computer has a microphone then select **Tools** > **Dictate Text** from the Editor Menu.

Speak clearly and naturally into the microphone. As you speak, the text will appear on the screen. Pronounce names of punctuation such as "period", "quote", and "question mark". Say "new paragraph" to start a new paragraph.

Click **Tools** > **Dictate Text** again to shut off the speech recognition.

> The speech recognition depends upon the Microsoft Windows operating system. If you are concerned about the dictation's accuracy, you can train Windows to understand better your voice. Search the Windows help for "speech recognition" for more details.

Fullscreen Editing

When writing, it is often helpful to remove all distractions so that you can better concentrate on composing the story. The computer screen itself can be a distraction.

To switch to Full Screen mode, select **View** > **Fullscreen**, click the **Fullscreen** button on the Composer Toolbar, or press **F11** on the keyboard. This will open the Composer to fill the entire computer screen to give you more area to work with. It also hides the Organizer, Editor Menu, Toolbar, and Status Bar.

When you are ready to save your story, click the **Fullscreen** button again or press **F11** to return to the regular-sized story editor.

How to Write Good

For the record- yes, I do know it should be "How to Write Well." But it illustrates an important point. Correct grammar isn't always necessary to communicate an idea or story. In fact, your grammatical mistakes may be an inseparable part of your personality and voice.

Let Your Voice Shine Through

Remember at the beginning when I asked you why you wanted to write a personal history? Many people write so that future generations will be able to know who they were. One of the greatest benefits of writing a personal history is the ability to preserve the life, the personality, and the voice of the subject.

Modern-day computers have sophisticated writing tools. In addition to perfect spelling, grammar checks can now make your writing grammatically flawless. But will it still sound like you?

> No matter what writing tips and tools you use, don't let them sanitize your personality out of your writing. Above all, let your voice shine through your writing.

I'm going to share some simple techniques to make your writing better. They're designed to make your stories clearer, more understandable, and more effective. However, be careful that whatever tricks you use, your writing still sounds natural and feels like "you."

Make it Readable

Don't try to impress people with the sophistication of your writing. Impress them with the simplicity, clarity and honest feelings that your writing conveys. The more difficult it is to read your history, the less likely that your family and others will be interested in reading it- or at least in finishing it.

How many personal histories have sat around for years without being read? Your goal should be to make your writing easy to read and interesting. Write something that will be read.

Personal Historian helps you to write in a way that people can read easily. The Readability Check (see page 119) can analyze what you have written and give you tips on how to make it more accessible to others.

Let's look at an example:

> I nervously walked up to her doorway, rang the doorbell, listened for any activity inside that would prepare me for what was to transpire, and waited as the door was opened by some unknown personage. I looked up to see her mother's animated face as she gestured me inside, and my shoulders were slouched as I entered and saw the whole family was there to inspect me. I nervously looked around, but Nancy couldn't be seen anywhere, but then I was relieved when I realized that she actually was there and was just hidden behind her mother. Then she quickly stepped forward, said goodbye to her family, and quickly walked out the door, and I followed after her.

A Readability Check shows us this:

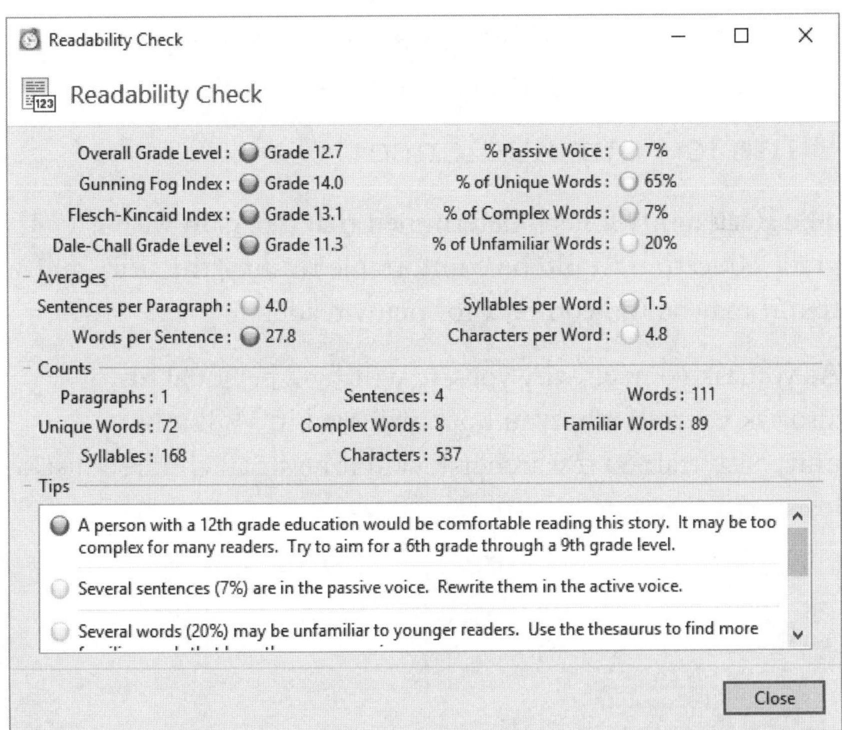

The check also gives us these tips to improve the writing:

- A person with a 12th grade education would be comfortable reading this story. It may be too complex for many readers. Try to aim for a 6th grade through a 9th grade level.
- Several sentences (7%) are in the passive voice. Rewrite them in the active voice.
- Several words (20%) may be unfamiliar to younger readers. Use the thesaurus to find more familiar words that have the same meaning.
- The average words per sentence (27.8) is a very high. Try breaking-up some sentences and aim for 15.0 to 20.0 words per sentence.
- The average characters per word (4.8) is a little high. Use the thesaurus to find shorter words that have the same meaning.

Let's apply some of the tips and see what happens.

Write to Your Audience

The Readability Check determined that a person with a 12th grade education would be comfortable reading the story and that it may be too complex for many readers.

As you ask yourself **why** you are writing a personal history, also ask yourself **who** you hope will read it. Will it be university-trained researchers? Will it be small children just learning to read?

When I imagine who I want to read my personal history, I imagine someone between the ages of 10 and 14 years old. I call this the "golden age." Someone old enough to understand my life experiences yet young enough not to have made many life-altering decisions. Someone who knows enough to learn but doesn't yet think they know everything.

> For this reason, I recommend that you aim for a grade level between 6 and 9. This will make your stories accessible not only to adults, but also to youth when they are young enough to get the most out of it.

Write with Strength

The Readability Check showed that several of our sentences were in the "passive voice". Passive means lacking energy or will. A passive sentence is one in which the subject of the sentence receives the action instead of giving it. It makes the sentence weak and uncertain and leaves us feeling that we are missing something.

For example, consider this:

The apple was eaten by John.

The subject of the sentence, “the apple”, was eaten. It didn’t do the eating. Since the subject and object are switched, a passive voice sentence can often be harder to follow-especially if there are many in a story.

The opposite of passive voice is “active voice”. In active voice, the subject does the acting.

John ate the apple.

The active voice sentence is much stronger and easier to understand.

Here’s a passage that is 100% passive voice:

> The chores were always done early in the morning by Luke. He was treated kindly by his wife, Alice, and by his daughter, Mary. In the mornings, he was pampered by his wife at breakfast time. In the evening, he was treated to songs by his daughter. The cows were milked before 6 o’clock by Luke, and the chickens were fed by him before 7.
>
> The fences were always mended by Luke within hours after the problem was discovered. Luke’s tractor was nearly always driven by him with great care.

This is the same passage in the active voice:

> Luke always did the chores early in the morning. His wife, Alice, and his daughter, Mary, treated him kindly. In the mornings, his wife pampered him at breakfast time. In the

evening, his daughter treated him to some songs. Luke milked the cows before 6 o'clock and fed the chickens by 7.

Luke always mended the fences within hours after he discovered the problem. Luke almost always drove his tractor with great care.

Can you feel the difference? They tell the same story and convey the same facts but one is much more readable than the other.

Our story has several uses of passive voice: "the door was opened by some unknown personage", "my shoulders were slouched", and "Nancy couldn't be seen anywhere".

We instantly make the story feel more lively by changing them to an active voice instead: "some unknown personage opened the door," "I slouched my shoulders", and "I couldn't see Nancy."

With little practice with the active voice, you will be writing more powerfully with sentences that have energy and will.

Finding the Right Word

The Readability Check found that 20% of our words might be unfamiliar to younger readers. We can use *Personal Historian's* thesaurus (see page 118) to find more familiar words that have the same meaning.

It also found that our words were a little big. We can also use the thesaurus to find shorter words that have the same meaning.

We can replace "transpire" with "come", "personage" with "person", "gestured" with "welcomed", and "animated" with "smiling".

We also notice that we overuse the words "nervous," "see," "look," and "quickly." The thesaurus helps us find some substitutions to add variety.

Shaking Things Up

The Readability Check found that the average words per sentence was very high. A high "average words per sentence" or a high "sentences per paragraph" makes the story feel long and drawn out. It's easily solved by breaking up some sentences with periods or separating some sentences into new paragraphs.

Our first sentence looks a little long. Let's break it up a little:

> I was nervous as I walked up to her door. I rang the doorbell, listening for any activity inside that would prepare me for what was to come. The door opened . . .

If you have the opposite problem (short sentences or paragraphs), the story can sound very choppy (think "The Cat in the Hat"). Fix that problem by combining sentences or paragraphs together.

The Difference

How does our story look now?

> I was nervous as I walked up to her door. I rang the doorbell, listening for any activity inside that would prepare me for what was to come. The door opened, and I looked up to see her mother's smiling face. She welcomed me into their home, and I slouched as I entered, realizing that the whole family was gathered there to inspect me.

I looked around but couldn't see any sign of Nancy. I was relieved to find that she hadn't run away and was actually there, just hiding behind her mom. She stepped forward, said goodbye to her family, and hurried out the door. I quickly followed after her, worried that she would reach the car before me.

Running this through the Readability Check gives much better results:

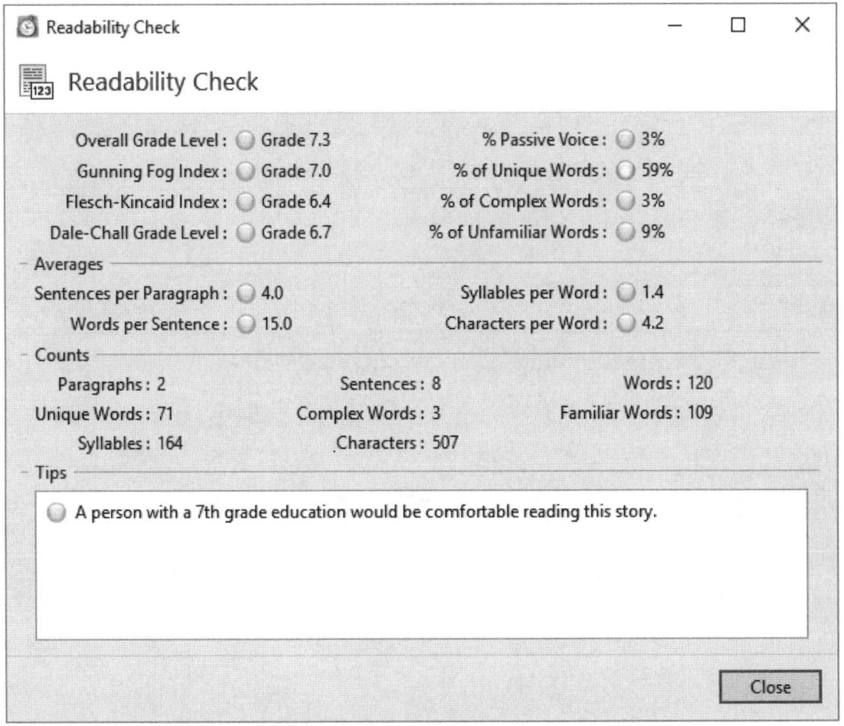

The Readability Check says, "A person with a 7th grade education would be comfortable reading this story."

The basic content of our story is the same. The original voice, personality, and feelings are all there. The difference is that it is now much easier to read and understand.

Do I Have Your Attention?

Your writing needs to be not just readable, but interesting as well. By "interesting", I don't mean full of pirates, adventure, and wizarding schools.

No matter how ordinary you feel your life is, don't underestimate how interesting it will be to future generations. If you've ever read old letters or journals, you'll understand that what was everyday and mundane to them can be fascinating to us today.

While our stories themselves may be interesting, the way we present them may not be.

In this chapter, you'll learn some tips and tricks to make your life stories exciting and vibrant, without having to resort to embellishment and exaggeration.

Show, Don't Tell

To hold a reader's attention, you need to "show" them what happened, not just "tell" them. It's the difference between "exposition" and "narration".

▶ Exposition

"Exposition" is to simply and directly tell the reader what happened. For example:

> Marcy had a hard time getting through the halls to the principal's office and was afraid she might be late. Yet she was hesitant to enter after she arrived at the door.

It does a good job of giving the basic facts, but it lacks the kinds of detail that help the reader visualize the environment.

▶ Narration

"Narration" takes the story beyond mere exposition. You should appeal to the reader's senses to describe characters and situations. You shows the reader everything that you want them to know, sense, or feel.

Let's look at our previous example with a touch of narration:

> As Marcy wove her way through the ocean of students, she often had to twist sideways to make herself fit through a

> small opening in the crowd. She often glanced quickly up at the hall clock as she constantly bumped from side to side. Finally, she arrived at the principal's door. She reached for the door knob, then quickly pulled her hand back. For just a moment she hesitated, just staring at the knob. She took a loud, deep breath. The suddenly, she grabbed the knob, turned it and walked through the door.

"Showing" the story through the senses and feelings will make your stories much more interesting that merely telling them what happened.

Add Context

It is not enough to write clearly and well to make a personal or family history interesting. It is also important that the reader is helped to see- and even feel- that the people in the history are (or were) living breathing people.

There are many ways to do this, but one of the most important is setting the history in context. Context is the collection of facts or circumstances that surround the event. It helps us to make sense of something. Context describes what conditions were like at the time an event happened. Therefore, context helps us to interpret that event.

As an example, suppose that we read the following in a personal history:

> The days were long for Ron. Puttering around the house had long since bored him almost to death. He had weeded the same garden, oiled the same hinges, cleaned the same tools, and repeated the same tasks time after time. He hated to see morning come.

Reading this, we wonder why he doesn't break the cycle of boredom and get a job or a hobby- something. What we don't know about Ron is the context of his life. Suppose we had been told that the Great Depression of the 1930's had struck Ron's town with a vengeance. Over 70 percent of the men in town were unemployed. Ron's skills were limited, and he had been in this condition for over two years. He had tried for many months to find work, but he was unsuccessful.

With this background, we understand Ron much better. He no longer seems like a lazy, shiftless man. Instead, he seems like a victim of his time. This is the purpose of context. It helps us put the history in perspective and see things and people more clearly; as they really were.

LifeCapsules are an easy way to add color and context to the history (see page 27). By importing LifeCapsules on subjects relevant to the person's life, you can gain perspective and insight that might not be possible otherwise.

What's a newspaper?

Have you ever read an old book or letter and seen a reference to a person, place, or thing that was obviously important but you had no idea what it was?

> Remember- what is obvious to you today may not be obvious to future generations. Make the effort to describe people, places, and things and why they were important.

For example, as a youth, I occasionally worked as a paperboy. I could write stories about delivering newspapers on my bike early in the morning and the things I learned.

My grandchildren may read these stories and think of several questions: Why was Grandpa throwing rolled up paper at homes early in the morning? Why would anybody pay him to do it? What's a "paperboy"? What's a "newspaper"?

In my story, I need to take the time to explain what a paperboy is and what my duties were. I need to explain why it was important and why people would pay for the service. With the way the world is changing, I should also explain what a newspaper is.

Let Your Characters Speak

I've been fortunate to read many life stories that have been shared with me. One thing that has surprised me is how many of them don't include actual dialogue. They refuse to let their characters speak.

What do I mean by "dialogue"? Compare these two examples. First, without dialogue:

> My mom asked me to ride my bike to the store and order a birthday cake. She said it was for my sister and that we were celebrating her birthday on July 25th instead of December 25th this year. I said sure and asked if I could use the extra money to go to a movie after the store. She said that was fine but not to buy any popcorn or candy.

Here's the same story with dialogue:

> "Could you please ride to the store and order a birthday cake?" my mom asked.
>
> "I guess," I replied. "Why?"

> "Well, I thought maybe we could surprise Katie with a party on July 25th this year. You know how she hates having a Christmas birthday."
>
> "She'll love that!" Hoping to cash in on my helpfulness, I added, "Could I use the change and go to a movie after the store?"
>
> She saw through my gambit but played along anyway. "Yeah, but no popcorn or candy. Got it?"

See the difference? Can you imagine reading an entire novel that had no actual dialogue- where all the conversations were indirectly described? Such a novel would be lifeless and boring, and you'd lose interest.

Adding dialogue instantly makes the characters come to life. It also gives them a voice and personality.

But what if you don't remember the conversation or exact words used? Write the dialogue anyway. This isn't a courtroom deposition. And if you don't provide the characters' words, the reader will be forced to imagine them.

Ask yourself who will do a better job of voicing the characters: you- the person who likely knew them personally- or an unknown future reader?

Give them the voice they deserve and bring your characters to life with dialogue.

Putting It All Together

So you've created your file. You've built your timeline. You've brainstormed and outlined each event and memory. You've written interesting and readable stories. Now is the time to finish off the last of the elephant. Now is the time to let *Personal Historian* bring it all together.

The *Personal Historian* Publisher gathers all the stories you've written into a single, finished history. You can even create multiple books using different stories and settings, all from a single file.

Creating a New Book

To create a new book, click the little arrow to the right of the **Book** Toolbar button on the Main Menu. A menu will appear.

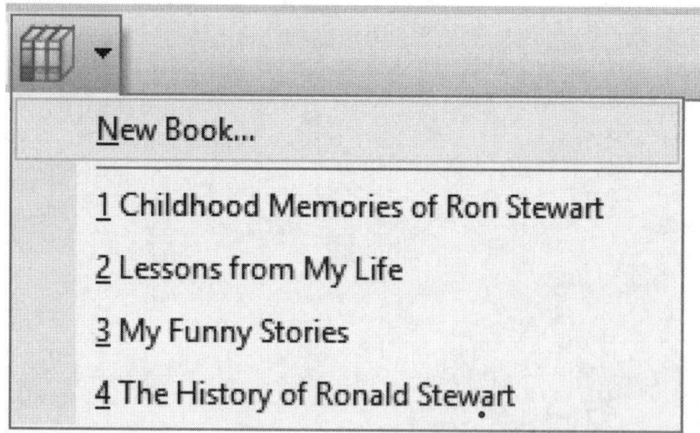

Select **New Book** to bring up the "Create a New Book" wizard. The wizard will guide you through the initial setup of your book.

▶ Book Information

The first step is to enter basic information for the book.

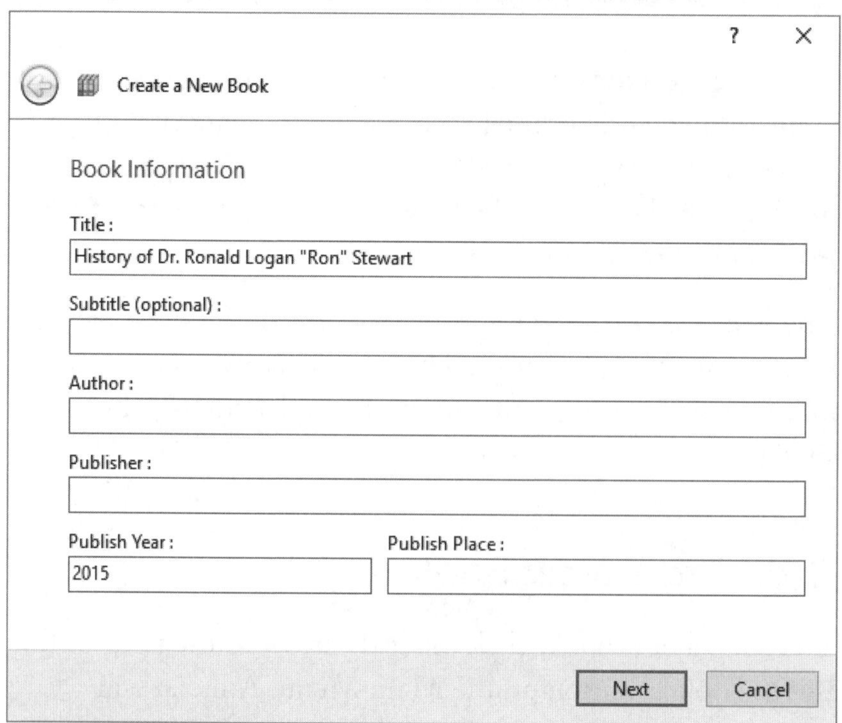

Enter the title, subtitle, author, and publisher information. Click **Next** to move on.

▶ Special Sections

You can then choose which special sections you would like to include in your published book.

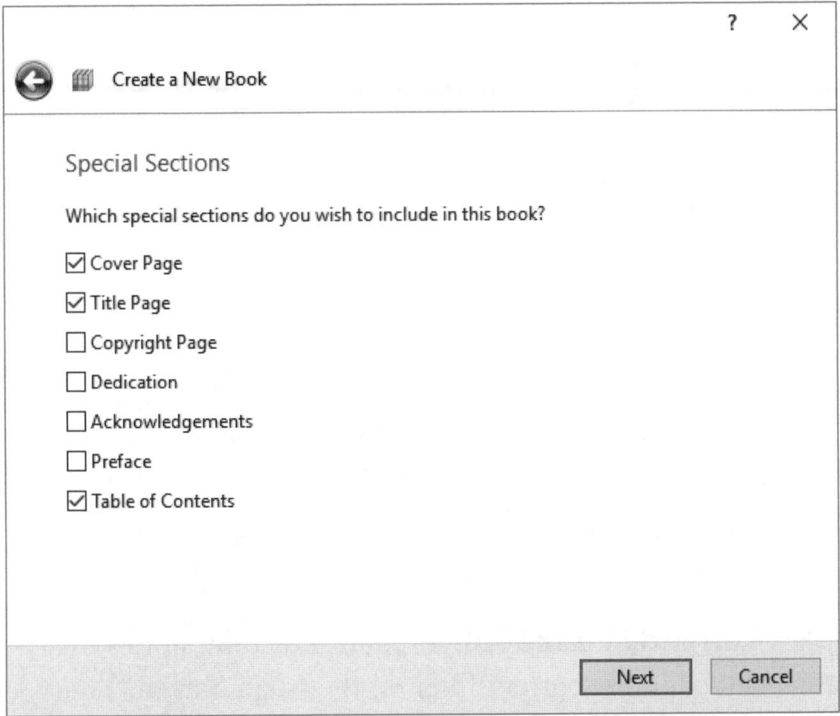

Choices include Cover Page, Title Page, Copyright Page, Dedication, Acknowledgements, Preface, and Table of Contents. Check the special sections you want and then click **Next**. You'll be able to customize each section later.

▶ Which stories do you wish to include?

The next step is to choose which stories to include in the book.

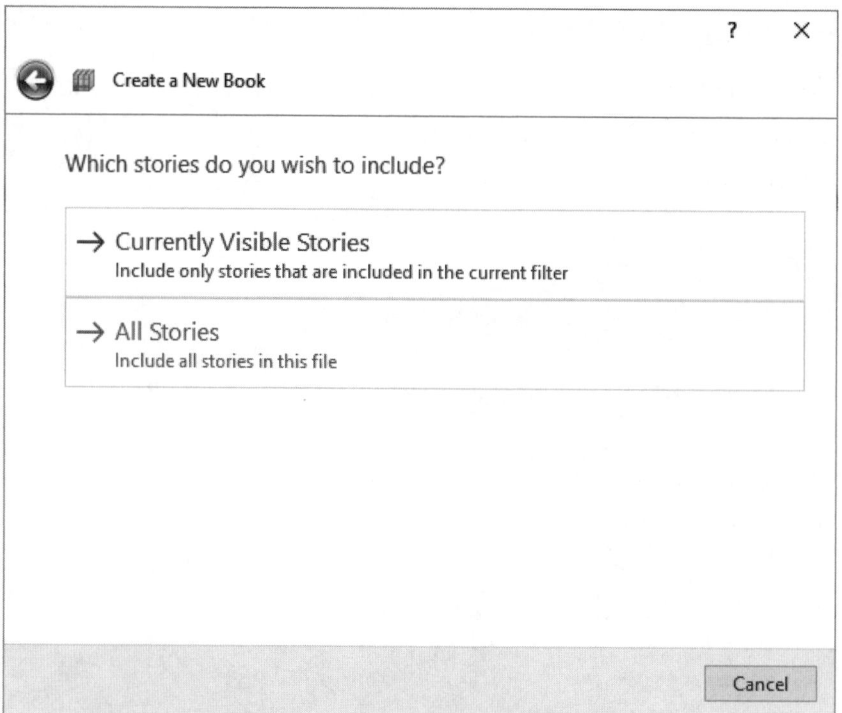

Choose **All Stories** to include all the stories in the file.

Click **Currently Visible Stories** to include only stories that are included in the current filter on the Main Screen. You could filter stories from specific categories, a certain time period, or many other criteria.

Maybe you want to leave out stories you have put in a "Private" category, or maybe you want only to include stories from your childhood. Or a book that only includes stories in a particular place.

See "Filtering Stories" on page 47 for more information on filtering stories.

▶ Chapters

The next step is to tell the wizard how you want to organize the stories into chapters.

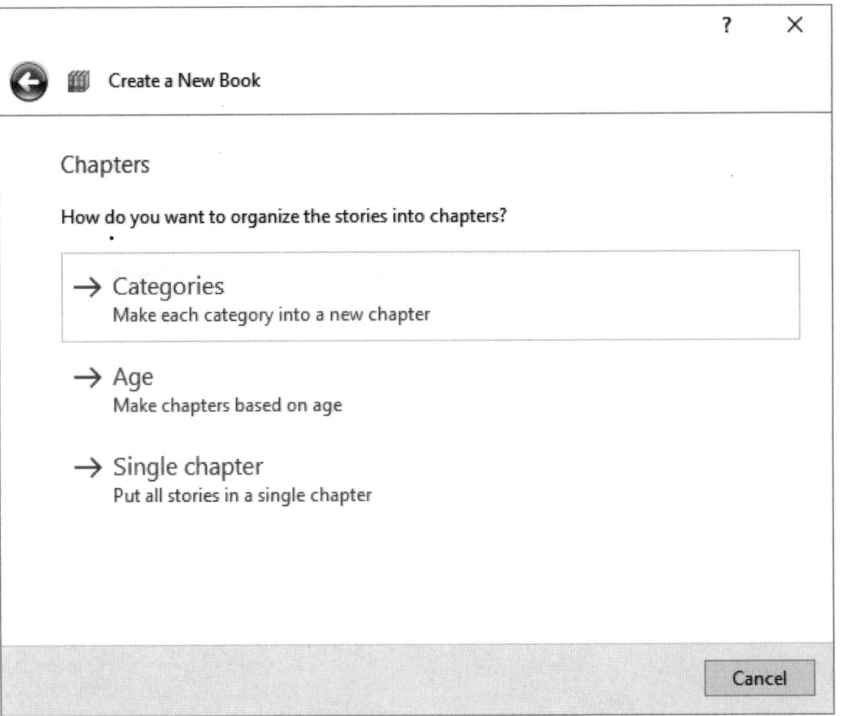

Click **Categories** to make each category into a new chapter. If you choose to organize your stories by category, *Personal Historian* will print the categories in the order you arrange them in (see "Changing the Order of Categories" on page 74). You can also rearrange the chapters (categories) in the Publisher after the wizard has finished.

Select **Single chapter** to put all the stories into one, single chapter.

Choose **Age** to make chapters based on age ranges. This option will display a new screen:

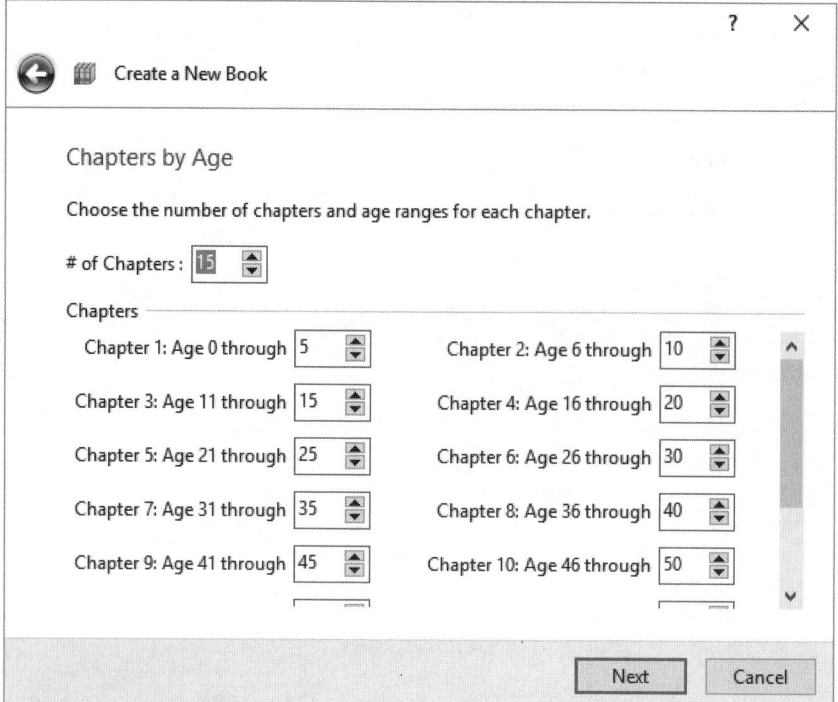

Tell *Personal Historian* the number of chapters you want. You may then tell it the exact range of ages to include in each chapter.

Click **Next** to continue.

▶ Book Options

The final wizard screen lets you select some basic options for the book.

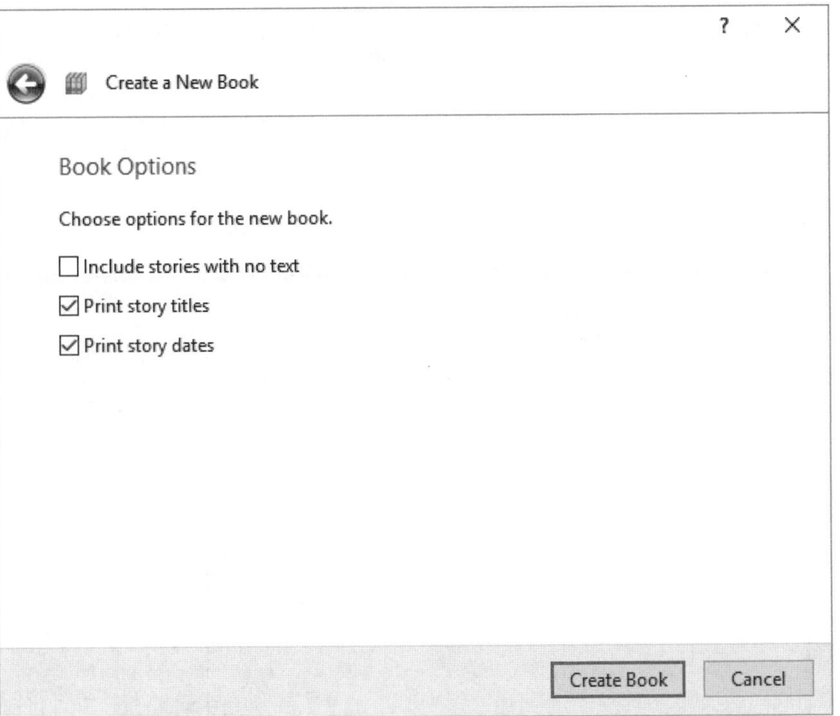

- **Include stories with no text** –print stories that are just placeholders and that don't contain any written story.
- **Print story titles** - print each story's title before its text.
- **Print story dates** - print each story's date or date range before its text.

Click **Create Book** to close the wizard and open the book in the Publisher (see page 150).

Managing Books

Personal Historian will let you create multiple books from a single file. To manage your books, select **Publish** > **Books** from the Main Menu or click the button on the Main Toolbar.

You will see a list of any books you have already created (or a message that there are no books yet).

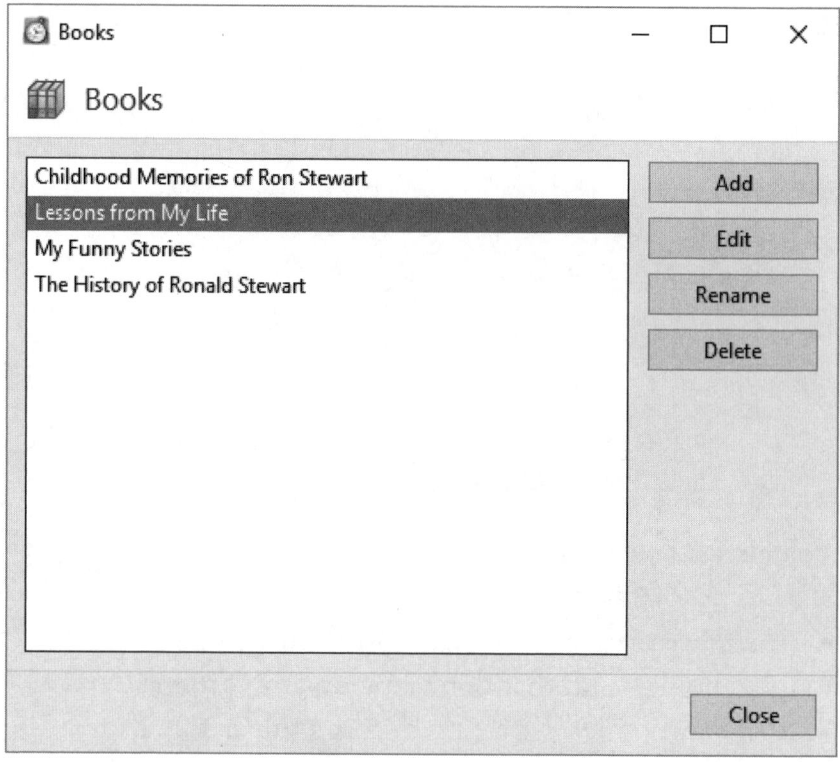

▶ Adding a New Book

To add a new book, click the **Add** button. *Personal Historian* will bring up the "Create a New Book" wizard (see page 141) to get the initial settings for your book. After you have completed the wizard, the Publisher will allow you to customize your personal history book.

▶ Editing an Existing Book

To edit an existing book, select it from the list and click the **Edit** button. *Personal Historian* will open the Publisher (see page 150) for the book where you can change its chapters and settings.

▶ Renaming an Existing Book

To rename a book, select it from the list and click the **Rename** button. An edit box with the current name will be displayed.

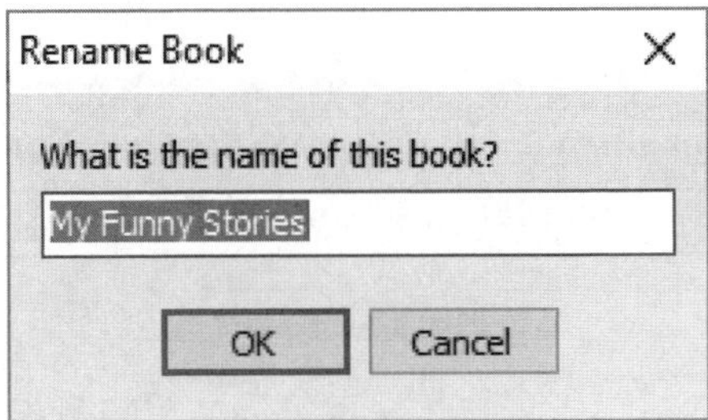

You can change the name and click **OK** to rename the book.

▶ Deleting an Existing Book

To delete a book, select it from the list and click the **Delete** button.

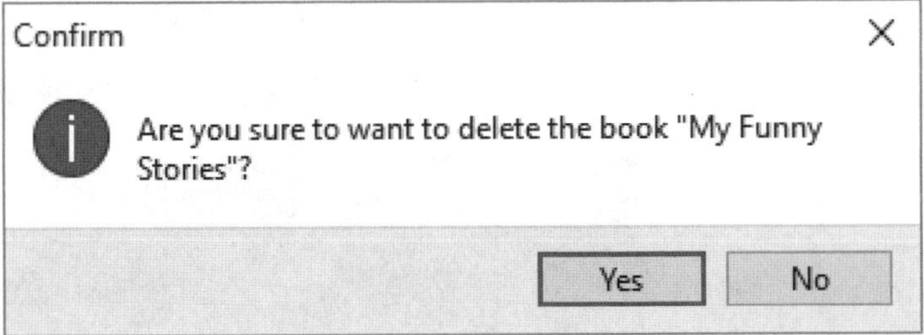

Click **Yes** to confirm that you do want to remove the book.

Using the Publisher

The Publisher is the heart of *Personal Historian's* book capability. This is where you add, edit, and rearrange the chapters of your book, and select your layout and other options.

The Publisher is shown after you've created a new book (see page 150) or have selected a book to edit (see page 148).

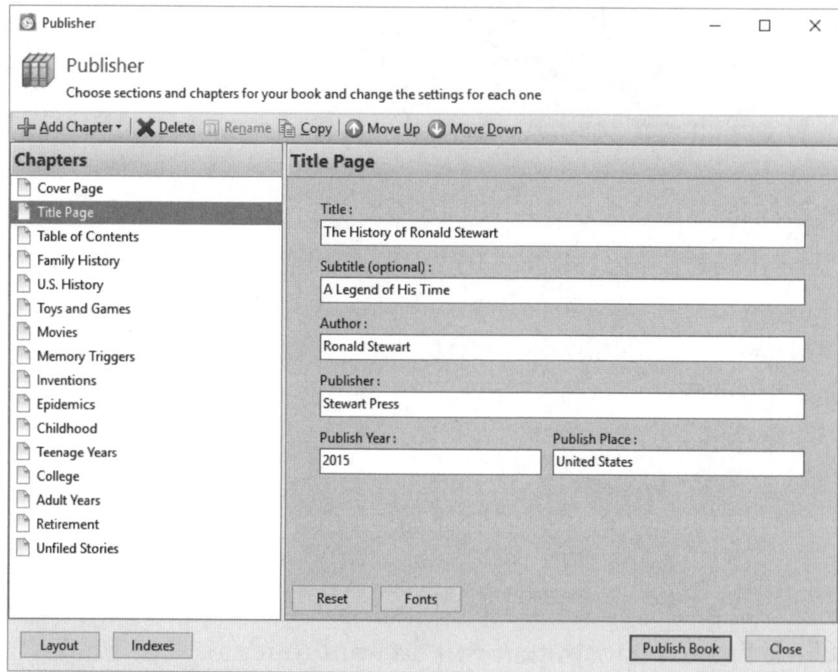

▶ Working with Chapters

To add a chapter to your book, click the **Add Chapter** button and select the type of chapter you want to add. *Personal Historian* will add it to the list on the left side of the page. Options for that chapter appear on the right.

You can add special chapter types like a cover page, title page, and table of contents. You can also add a group of stories as a chapter within your book.

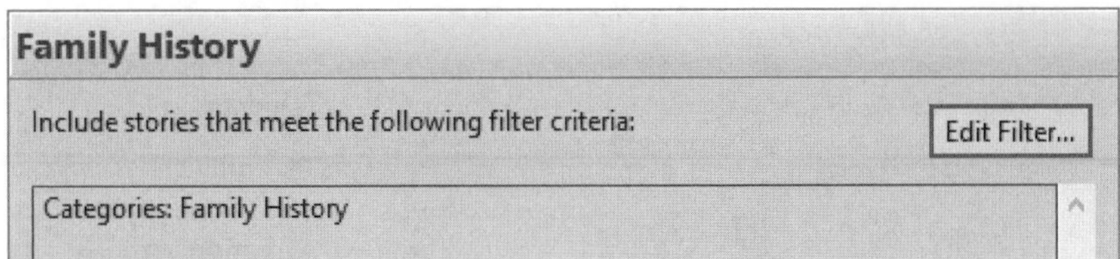

A chapter of stories will have an **Edit Filter** button. Click this to choose which stories will appear in that chapter. You can filter stories based on the person's age, categories, places, people, and more (seeon page 49).

You can rearrange the chapters in a book by clicking and dragging a story in the list up or down, or by clicking the **Move Up** and **Move Down** buttons on the Publisher.

You can delete a chapter by highlighting the chapter name and clicking the **Delete** button. You will be asked to confirm that you want to remove the chapter.

You can rename a chapter by highlighting the chapter name and clicking the **Rename** button. An edit box will appear where you can change the name.

If you want to make a copy of a chapter, highlight the chapter name and click the **Copy** button. This lets you create a chapter that is similar to another chapter without having to reinvent it completely.

▶ Modifying the Page Layout

Personal Historian allows you full control over the layout of the book. Click the **Layout** button on the Publisher to see the "Page Layout" screen.

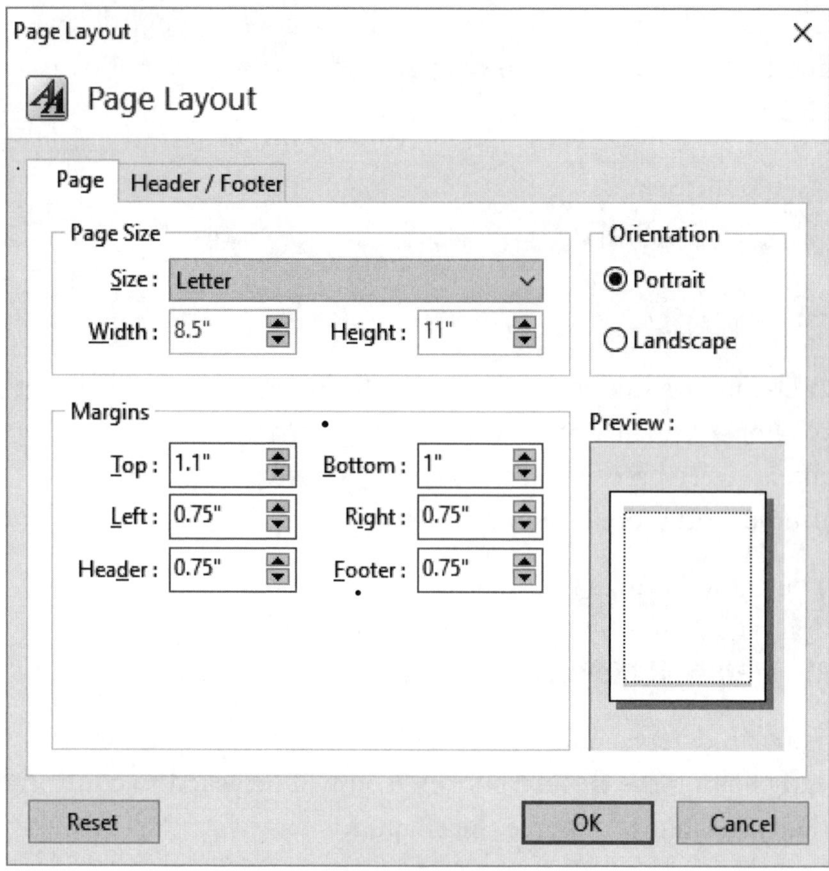

Here you can modify the page size, margins, and header and footer.

▶ Adding Indexes

The Publisher can also add indexes to the end of your book. Click the **Indexes** button on the Publisher to see the "Index Settings" screen.

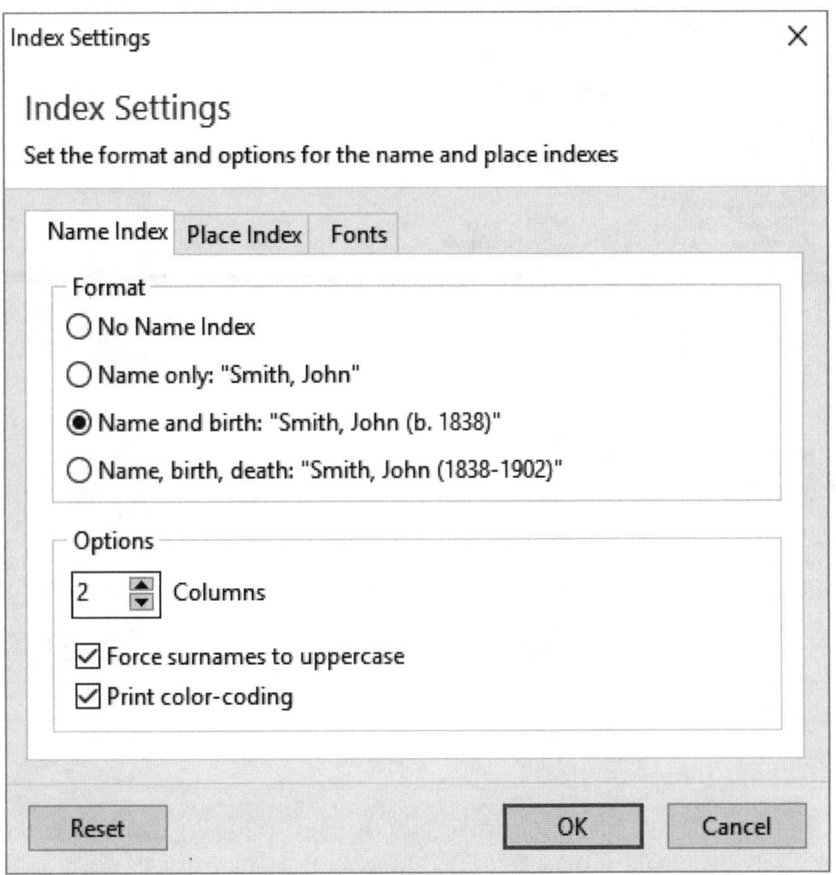

You can add an index of names (see "Recording People" on page 75) and an index of places (see "Tracking Places" on page 81). You can also set columns, fonts, and other options from this screen.

Printing and Exporting Your Work

When you have your book and chapters set-up just how you want them, click the **Publish Book** button to see the book. The Report Viewer will appear.

▶ Report Viewer

The Report Viewer shows you what your book will look like on paper.

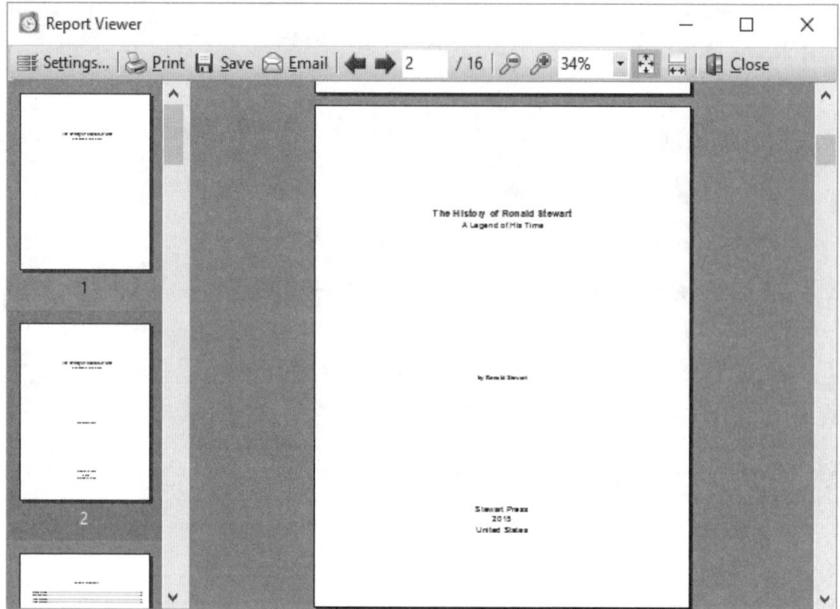

On the left is a list of thumbnails of each page in the book. You can use the arrow keys or the scroll bar to scroll through each page in the book, or you can use the mouse to scroll down (or up) and go to the desired page.

> The page numbers in the Table of Contents and the Indexes have links to the respective page, and clicking on the page number will take you directly to that page.

The Report Viewer Toolbar has several buttons and boxes to help you work with the book:

- **Settings** – Make adjustments to the current book's settings.

- **Print** – Allows you to print the book you are currently viewing. *Personal Historian* will bring up the print options dialog.
- **Save** – Create an Acrobat PDF, Rich Text Format (RTF), Web page (HTML), or text file (TXT) from the book.
- **Email** – Send a copy of the book in Acrobat PDF, Rich Text Format (RTF), Web page (HTML), or text file (TXT) to another person via email.
- **Previous** – Displays the page before the currently displayed one.
- **Next** – Displays the page after the currently displayed one.
- **GoTo** – Type in the page number you wish to view and press Enter.
- **Zoom Out** – Zooms out of the document to show you more of the overall look of the document.
- **Zoom In** – Zooms in on the document to show you more detail.
- **Zoom Level** – Type in the zoom level % at which you wish to view the document and press Enter, or you can click on the down arrow to select from the preset zoom levels.
- **Fit Full Page** – Zoom the document so that an entire page fits on the screen.
- **Fit Page Width** – Zoom the document so that the width of the page fits on the screen.
- **Close** – Closes the report viewer.

▶ Save Report

When you click **Save**, *Personal Historian* will prompt you for the format to save it in.

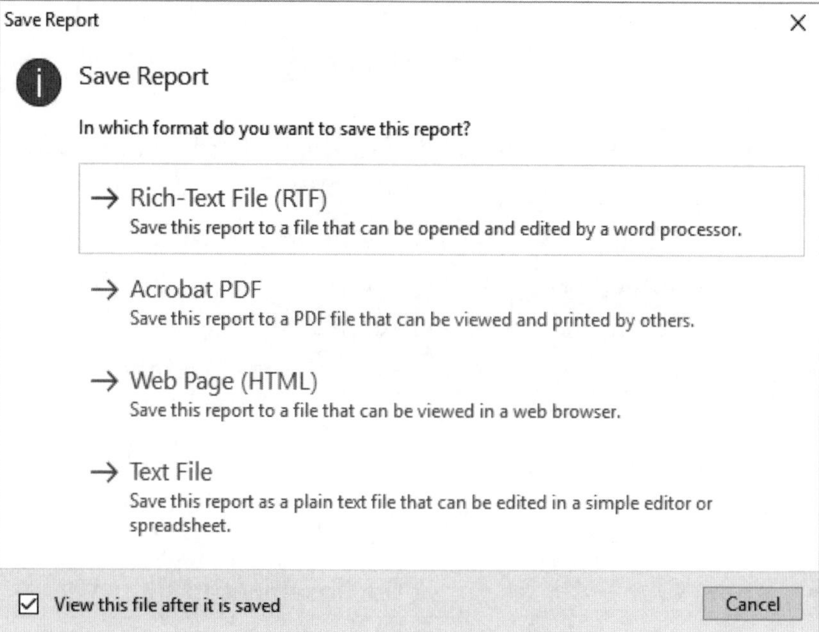

You may choose from:

- **Rich-Text File (RTF)** – Save this report to a file that can be opened and edited by a word processor.
- **Acrobat PDF** – Save this report to a PDF file that can be viewed and printed by others.
- **Web Page (HTML)** – Save this report to a file that can be viewed in a web browser.
- **Text File** – Save this report as a plain text file that can be opened in a simple editor or spreadsheet.

By checking **View this file after it is saved**, *Personal Historian* will automatically open the file with its associated program after saving is complete.

▶ Email Report

Personal Historian can send a copy of the book to your desktop email program, making it easy to send as an email attachment. When you click **Email**, *Personal Historian* will prompt you for the format to email.

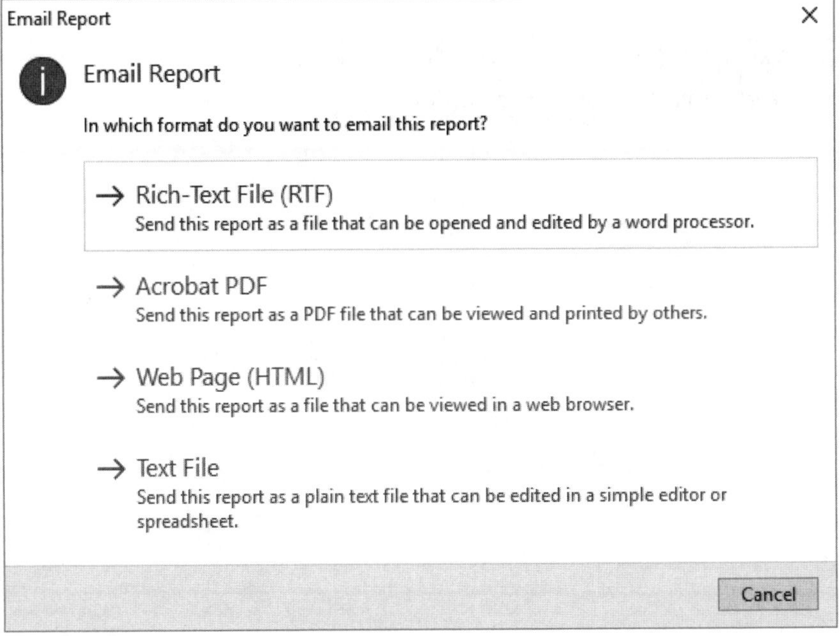

You have the same format choices as when you save the file to disk (see page 155).

> To use this feature, you must have a MAPI-enabled email program on a Windows computer such as Outlook, Outlook Express, Windows Mail, Eudora, etc. See your email program's documentation to make sure that it supports MAPI. This feature will not work with web-based email services such as AOL, Yahoo, Hotmail, or Gmail.

Publishing a Single Story

To print or export an individual story, you must first open the story in the Editor Screen (see page 87).

Select **File** > **Print/Export**. From the Editor Menu, click the **Print/Export** button on the Editor Toolbar, or press **Ctrl** + **P** on the keyboard.

The story will appear in the Report Viewer where it may be printed, saved to file, or emailed.

Protecting Your Work

It's heartbreaking for me to hear stories of people who have spent countless hours working on their personal histories only to lose everything through an unexpected software, hardware, or human failure.

It's even more heartbreaking when I hear from a family member who has lost irreplaceable work left by a loved one who has passed away.

These tragedies are completely preventable if you will follow a few basic rules:

1. Backup your data often
2. Keep past backups, not just the latest
3. Keep backups in multiple places

Rule #1: Backup your data often

Personal Historian makes it easy to backup your data. In fact, each time that you close a file or exit the software, it will ask you if you want to make a backup of your data.

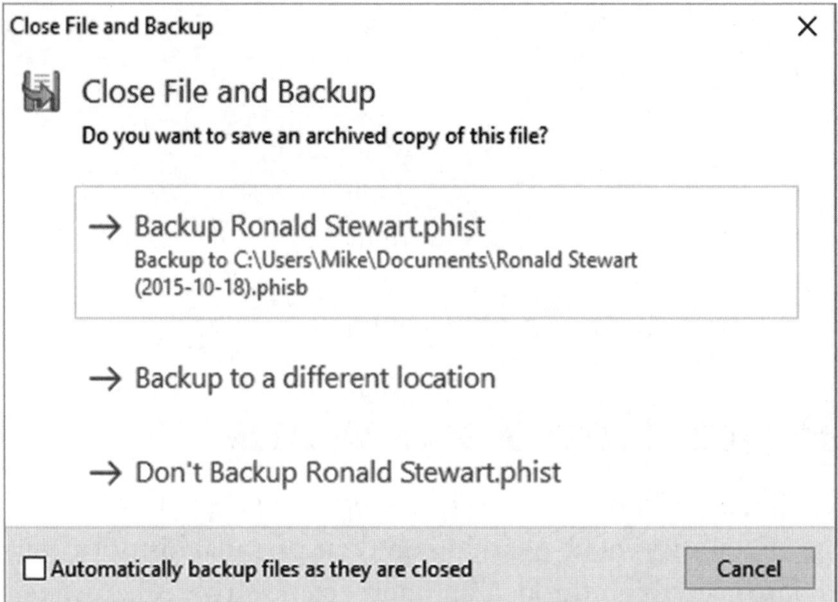

To backup to the default backup folder, click **Backup**. The backup will be a compressed version of your file and its name will end with ".phisb".

Click **Backup to a different location** if you would like to choose a different drive or folder. You can change the default backup folder in the Program Options (see page 169).

If you're a risk-taker and are feeling lucky, click **Don't Backup**.

Check **Automatically backup files as they are closed** to tell *Personal Historian* to always backup your file when you close it.

> You can backup your data at any time by selecting **File** > **Backup** from the Main Menu.

Rule #2: Keep past backups, not just the latest

Simply backing up your data isn't always enough. For example, I once spoke with a *Personal Historian* user who noticed several of her stories were missing from her file. Realizing that she had mistakenly deleted the stories a few days before, she nervously restored her file from her backup.

You can imagine her disappointment when she saw that the restored file was also missing the stories. The backup was made after she had made the mistake and before she realized what she had done.

Unfortunately, she was in the habit of only keeping one backup; overwriting her last backup every time she made a new one. Because of this, she could not recover her deleted stories.

→ Backup Ronald Stewart.phist
Backup to C:\Users\Mike\Documents\Ronald Stewart (2015-10-18).phisb

By default, *Personal Historian* will add the date to the end of the backup file's name. Using this feature allows you to keep a daily backup of your work.

If you discover that there is a problem in your file, you can "go back in time" and restore a backup from a date before the problem began.

Rule #3: Keep backups in multiple places

I'm sometimes asked, "Where should I keep my backups? On my hard drive? On a CD? Online?" My answer: "Yes."

You know the saying, "Don't put all your eggs in one basket"?

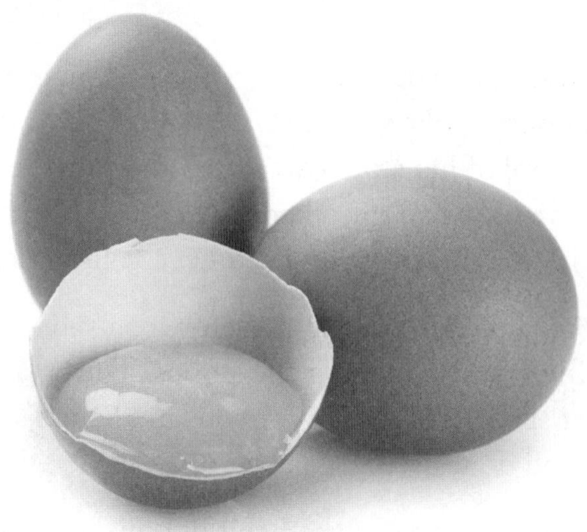

You could also say, "Don't put all your backups in one place." Just as keeping your eggs in a single basket puts you at risk of dropping the basket and breaking all your eggs, keeping your backups in a single place puts you at risk of losing them.

The best backup strategy is to have multiple strategies. Any hard drive, flash drive, CD, or online service is vulnerable to failure, destruction, and disaster.

Use as many of these backup methods as you can. Many online backup services such as Backblaze, Carbonite, Dropbox, or Mozy will keep the file both on your computer hard drive and online.

Send copies of your work to family members so it is safely kept in a variety of physical locations.

That way, if you drop one basket, you'll still have eggs safely protected in other baskets.

Restoring from a Backup

If the time ever comes that you need to recover your work from a backup, *Personal Historian* makes it easy.

To restore a file from a backup, select **File** > **Restore** from the Main Menu. The "Restore *Personal Historian* from Backup" wizard will appear.

▶ Where is the backup of the file you wish to restore?

It first asks if you know where your backup file is.

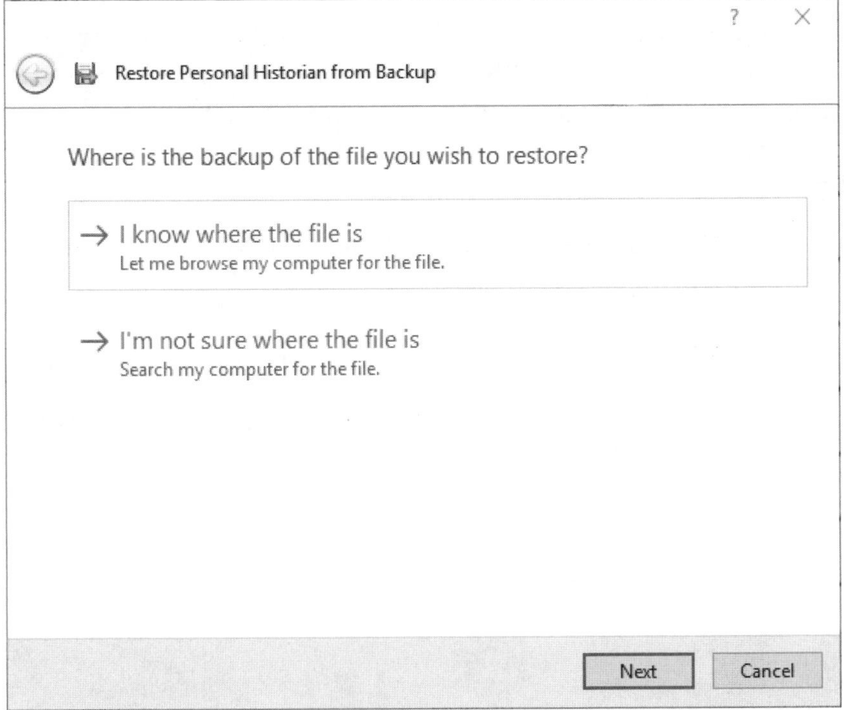

Click **I know where the file is** if you do. Click **I'm not sure where the file is** if you're not an alien superintelligence and need the software to search your computer for your file.

Select the file you want and then click **Open**.

▶ To where would you like to place the restored file?

The final step is to choose the name of the restored *Personal Historian* file. By default, this is the original name of the file that was backed up.

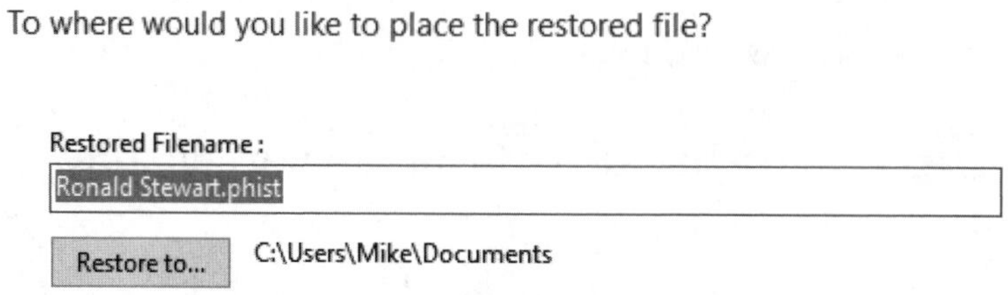

To where would you like to place the restored file?

Restored Filename :

Ronald Stewart.phist

Restore to... C:\Users\Mike\Documents

> When you restore a file, it will replace any changes that were made to the file since the backup. If you wish to keep the original file, you must give the restored file a different filename.

Click **Restore to** if you want to change the location of the restored file.

Click **Restore** to complete the file restoration.

After *Personal Historian* restores the backup, it will open the newly restored file.

Good Luck

You made it!

That means that you've read this book and:

1. learned about the obstacles that prevent us from writing histories
2. discovered how to use *Personal Historian* to overcome those obstacles
3. read valuable tips on how to make your writing clearer and more interesting
4. saw how *Personal Historian* pulls it all together to publish a book

Or you just skipped ahead to this page. If so, go back to page 1 and don't cheat this time. I'll wait right here.

So now that you're here, I hope that you're excited to finally make progress on your life stories. I hope you're inspired with tips and ideas on how to write engaging stories. Most of all, I hope you're confident that you can fulfill the reasons why you are writing a personal history.

Good luck!

You're still here?

It's over!

Go home!

Go!

Reference Guides

Program Options

There are some options that affect the program as a whole. These include general options, display options, and the default folders for various types of files. To change the program options, from the Main Menu, select **Tools** > **Program Options**.

▶ General Options

General options let you change some settings that affect the general operation of *Personal Historian*.

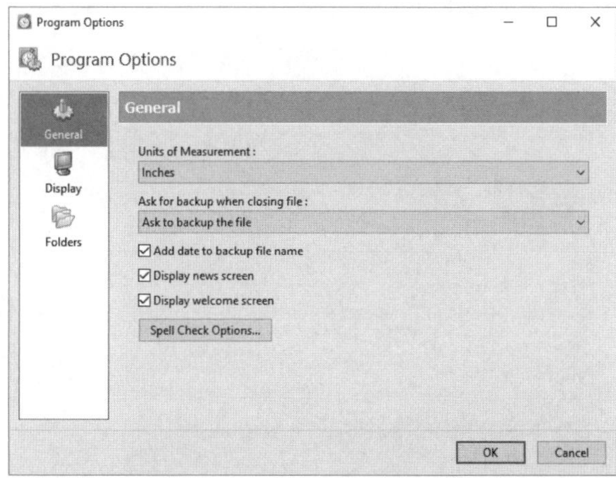

Units of Measurement - Switch between using inches and centimeters

Ask for backup when closing file - Choose whether *Personal Historian* should ask to back up your file when you close it, just back it up without asking, or not back it up.

Add date to backup file name - Tell *Personal Historian* whether you want it to add the current date to the backup file name. This allows you to keep multiple backups of your file over time.

Display news screen - Choose whether *Personal Historian* should display the News Screen at startup.

Display welcome screen - Choose whether *Personal Historian* should display the Welcome Screen at startup.

Spell Check Options - Set various spell check options, like which dictionary to use.

▶ Display Options

Display options let you customize the look and feel of the *Personal Historian* screens.

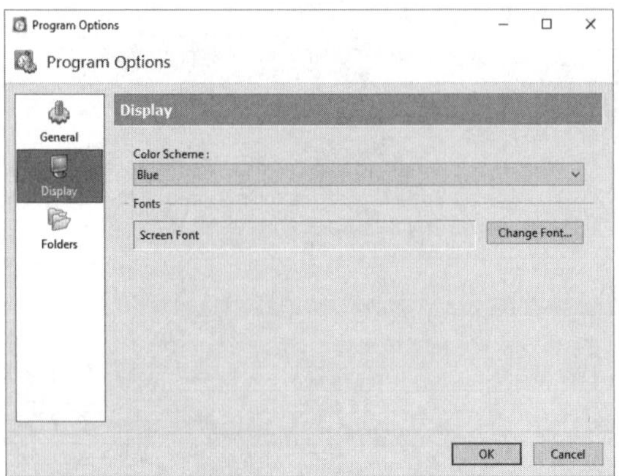

You can choose a color scheme and the font to use on screens.

▶ Folders

The Folders section lets you set the default folders for various types of files.

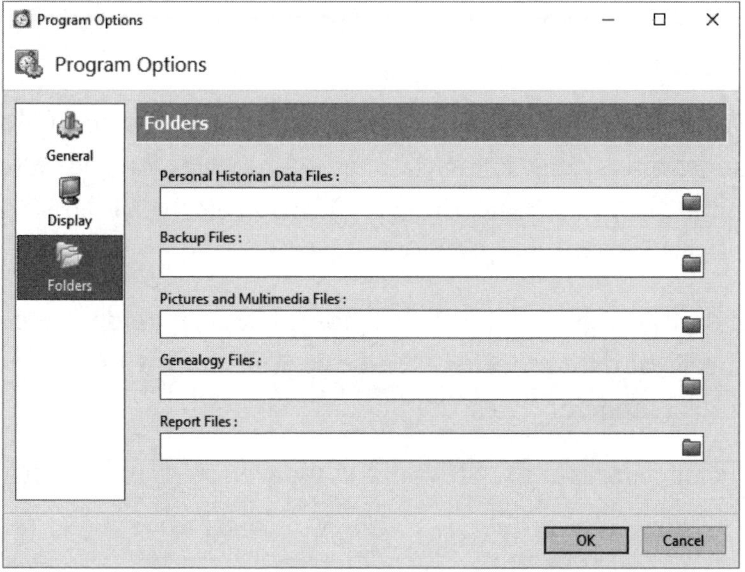

You can click the little folder button at the right of each box to select the folder. *Personal Historian* will then use the folder you select as the default when saving or loading that particular file type.

Dates and Ages

It would be impossible to work with histories without dealing with dates or ages. *Personal Historian* supports a rich variety of date and age formats, allowing you to record, filter, and organize your stories.

▶ Dates

Personal Historian uses dates in several of its functions (file options, filters, importing data, editing stories, etc.) It also automatically computes the day of the week for all dates from 1753 and beyond.

The dates can be complete or incomplete, can be described with several date modifiers, and can even, in most cases, include a range of dates.

You can even use "BC" if you are lucky enough to have lived that long.

Examples include:

- 1955
- Jul 1955
- July 1955
- 17 July ????
- 17 July 1955
- July 17, 1955
- 7/17/55
- 7-17-55
- 17 ??? 1955

Double Dates

Personal Historian also supports double dates, used in many countries before the adoption of the Gregorian calendar. You would enter these double dates with a slash separating the two years, like "13 Feb 1729/30".

Quaker Dates

Personal Historian has built-in date support for Quaker dates. Quaker dates are written referring to days of the weeks and months of the year by their number, rather their "pagan" god names.

Personal Historian accepts these dates as "12day 5month 1588" or "12da 5mo 1588", and displays them as "12da 5mo 1588." Note that Quaker dates before 1752 were based on the Julian calendar, so the first month refers to March, not January.

British Quarter Dates

Personal Historian also supports British quarter dates. The quarter date is commonly found in birth, marriage, and death records (BMD) from the United Kingdom. Quarter dates are written out as follows:

- Mar Q 1880 = Between 1 Jan and 31 Mar 1880
- Jun Q 1880 = Between 1 Apr and 30 Jun 1880
- Sep Q 1880 = Between 1 Jul and Sep 30 1880
- Dec Q 1880 = Between 1 Oct and 31 Dec 1880

▶ Ages

Personal Historian uses ages in several of its functions (filters, importing data, editing stories, etc.)

> To use ages, a birth date (or estimated birth date) of the individual(s) must be set in the file options (see page 58).

The ages can be complete or incomplete, can be described with several age modifiers, and can even, in most cases, include a range of ages.

Age Formats

Personal Historian can recognize a wide variety of age formats. The years, months, weeks, and even the days of an age are optional. Examples include:

- 18 years
- 18 y
- 18 years 3 months 2 weeks 3 days
- 18 y 3 m 2 w 3 d
- 18 y, 3 m, 17 days

▶ Ranges

Most dates and ages in *Personal Historian* can include a range. Examples include:

Range	Description	Example
Before	Before a date	before 17 Jul 1955
By	Happened by this date	by 17 Jul 1955
To	End date of an unknown period	to 17 Jul 1955
Until	Until a date	until 17 Jul 1955
From	Start date of an unknown period	from 17 Jul 1955
Since	Since a date	since 17 Jul 1955
After	After a date	after 17 Jul 1955
Between/And	A date which is between two dates.	between 17 Jul 1955 and 18 Jul 1955
From/To	A date period. Useful for spans like the time period a person held an occupation.	from 17 Jul 1955 to 18 Jul 1955
- (dash)	Date period	17 Jul 1955-18 Jul 1955

Range	Description	Example
Or	Conflicting dates	17 Jul 1955 or 18 Jul 1955

▶ Modifiers

You can modify a date or age with a word to add important information such as "About," "After," "Before," "Calculated," and "Estimated." Examples include:

Modifier	Description	Example
About	Near a date	abt 17 Jul 1955
Estimate	An estimated date	est 17 Jul 1955
Calculated	A calculated date	calc 17 Jul 1955
Circa	Near a date	ca 17 Jul 1955
Say	An estimated date	say 17 Jul 1955
Certainly	Little doubt about the date	cert 17 Jul 1955
Probably	More than likely date	prob 17 Jul 1955
Possibly	Some evidence supports the date	poss 17 Jul 1955
Likely	Odds favor the date	lkly 17 Jul 1955
Apparently	Presumed date	appar 17 Jul 1955
Perhaps	Could be the date	prhps 17 Jul 1955
Maybe	Date might be correct	maybe 17 Jul 1955

Menu Commands

This section provides a brief description of each command in the various menus. Also, the page number is provided where you will find more details about the feature.

▶ Main Menu Commands

File

Command	Description	Page
New	Create a new file	15
Open	Open an existing file	54
Open Recent	Choose from list of recent file	
Search for Files	Search computer for files	54
Close	Close currently opened file	
Rename	Move or rename a file	55
Delete	Delete a file	55
Copy	Create a copy of a file	56
Import		
Import Genealogy	Import a genealogy file	21
Import LifeCapsule	Import a LifeCapsule or timeline	27
Import Text Data	Import other text data	32

Command	Description	Page
Convert Version 1	Convert an old *Personal Historian* version 1 file	
Backup	Make a backup of your file	159
Restore	Restore your file from a backup	163
Properties	See file properties and fix errors	57
Exit	Exit the program	

View

Command	Description	Page
Filter	Filter stories by criteria	47
Remove Filter	Remove filter from stories	50
Saved Filters		
Save Filter	Save the current filter	50
Organize Filters	Add, edit, or delete saved filters	50
List Layout	Edit columns of the story list	44
Time Slider	Hide/show the Time Slider	39
Sidebar	Hide/show the Sidebar	48
Story Details	Hide/show the Story Details	39

Stories

Command	Description	Page
Add Story	Add a new story	65

Command	Description	Page
Delete Stories	Delete selected stories	67
Edit Story	Edit the selected story	65
Edit Random Story	Pick a story at random to edit	65
Add Journal Entry	Add a new story with today's date	67
Categories	Add, edit, and delete categories	69
People	Add, edit, and delete people	75
Places	Add, edit, and delete places	81

Publish

Command	Description	Page
Books	Manage and publish books	147
New Book	Create a new book	141

Tools

Command	Description	Page
Gazetteer	Lookup places around the world	
File Options	Edit the file's subject, author, and font styles	58
Program Options	Adjust general, display, and folder settings	167

Help

Command	Description	Page
Contents	Show the help file	
Check for Updates	Check for program updates over the internet	
Personal Historian News	Show news about *Personal Historian* from the internet	
Learning Center	Open a webpage to learn how to use *Personal Historian*	
Technical Support	Open a webpage to learn how to get technical support	
Register *Personal Historian*	Register your copy of *Personal Historian*	
About *Personal Historian*	See software version number and information	

▶ Editor Screen Menu Commands

File

Command	Description	Page
Save	Save story	
Save and Close	Save story and close Edit Screen	
Print/Export	Print or export the story	157
Import	Import a document into story	115
Close	Close the Edit Screen	

Edit

Command	Description	Page
Undo	Undo the last change	
Redo	Redo the last change	
Cut	Cut text to the clipboard	
Copy	Copy text to the clipboard	
Paste	Paste text & pictures from the clipboard	
Select All	Select all the text	
Delete	Delete selected text	
Find	Find text in the story	
Replace	Find and replace text in the story	

View

Command	Description	Page
Fullscreen	Toggle fullscreen mode	123
Organizer	Show/hide the Organizer	91

Format

Command	Description	Page
Styles	Add or edit font style	110
Bold	**Bold** selected text	
Italic	*Italicize* selected text	
Underline	Underline selected text	

Command	Description	Page
Strikethrough	~~Strikethrough~~ selected text	
Subscript	Subscript selected text	
Superscript	Superscript selected text	
Clear Formatting	Clear all formatting for the selected text	
Align Text Left	Align text to the left	
Center Text	Center text	
Align Text Right	Align text to the right	
Justify Text	Fully justify the text	

Insert

Command	Description	Page
Symbol	Insert a symbol or international character	
Picture	Add a picture to the text	112
Footnote	Insert a footnote	
Horizontal Line	Insert a horizontal line	
Page Break	Insert a page break	

Organizer

Command	Description	Page
Add Item	Add a new item	94
Add Subitem	Add a new subitem	94
Move Left	Move selected items left	95
Move Right	Move selected items right	95
Move Up	Move selected items up	95
Move Down	Move selected items down	95
Copy to Composer	Copy items and subitems to the Composer	96

Tools

Command	Description	Page
Spell Check	Perform a spell check	117
Thesaurus	Show the thesaurus	118
Readability Check	Perform a Readability Check	119
Read to Me	Have the computer read the story back to you	122
Dictate Text	Use speech recognition to dictate text	122
Live Spell Check	Turn live spell check on or off	116
Configure Spell Check	Change spell check settings	118

Keyboard Shortcut Keys

There are shortcut keys on most *Personal Historian* screens. Pressing the **Alt** key will cause an underlined letter to appear on buttons and menu items. While holding **Alt** key, press the underlined letter on the keyboard to trigger the command.

There are also shortcut keys for the most commonly-used menu items on the various screen. Learning to use these shortcut keys can save you time and mouse movements.

▶ Main Screen Shortcut Keys

Shortcut	Description	Page
Ctrl+N	Create a new file	15
Ctrl+O	Open an existing file	54
Ctrl+F	Apply a filter to the story list	47
Shift+Ctrl+F	Remove the filter from the story list	50
Shift+Enter	Add a new story	65
Ctrl+Del	Delete the selected stories	67
Ctrl+Enter	Edit the selected story	65
Alt+Enter	Edit a random story	65
Ctrl+J	Add a journal entry	67
F1	Show help	

▶ Editor Shortcut Keys

Shortcut	Description	Page
Ctrl+S	Save story	
Ctrl+Alt+S	Save story and close Edit Screen	
Ctrl+P	Print or export the story	157
Ctrl+O	Import a document into story	115
Ctrl+Z	Undo the last change	
Ctrl+Y	Redo the last change	
Ctrl+X	Cut text to the clipboard	
Ctrl+C	Copy text to the clipboard	
Ctrl+V	Paste text & pictures from the clipboard	
Ctrl+A	Select all the text	
Ctrl+Del	Delete selected text	
Ctrl+F	Find text in the story	
Ctrl+H	Find and replace text in the story	
F11	Toggle fullscreen mode	123
Shift+Ctrl+S	Add or edit font style	110
Ctrl+B	**Bold** selected text	
Ctrl+I	*Italicize* selected text	
Ctrl+U	Underline selected text	
Ctrl+=	$_{\text{Subscript}}$ selected text	

Shortcut	Description	Page
Shift+Ctrl+=	Superscript selected text	
Ctrl+L	Align text to the left	
Ctrl+E	Center text	
Ctrl+R	Align text to the right	
Ctrl+J	Fully justify the text	
Ctrl+Alt+F	Insert a footnote	
F7	Perform a spell check	117
Shift+F7	Show the thesaurus	118
Alt+F7	Perform a Readability Check	119

▶ Organizer Shortcut Keys

Shortcut	Description	Page
Enter	Add a new item	94
Shift+Enter	Add a new subitem	94
Delete	Delete selected items	94
F2	Edit item	94
Alt+Left	Move selected items left	95
Alt+Right	Move selected items right	95
Alt+Up	Move selected items up	95
Alt+Down	Move selected items down	95
+ (Numeric Keypad)	Expand an item	94

Shortcut	Description	Page
- (Numeric Keypad)	Collapse an item	94
***** (Numeric Keypad)	Expand an item and its subitems	94
/ (Numeric Keypad)	Collapse an item and its subitems	94
Ctrl+X	Cut items to the clipboard	
Ctrl+C	Copy items to the clipboard	
Ctrl+Y	Paste items from the clipboards	

Index

D

E

F

N

O

P

Q

R

S

T

U

V

W

Z